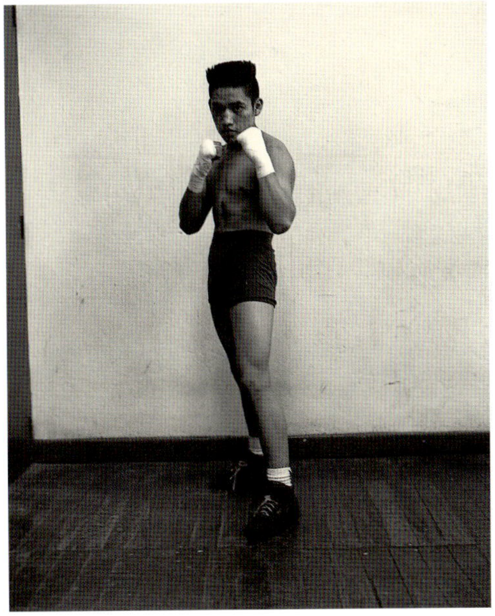

BOXERS

PHOTOGRAPHS & INTRODUCTIONS BY

KURT MARKUS

■

BOXING SHORTS BY

WALTER KIRN

■

EXCERPTS BY

NELSON ALGREN

LEONARD GARDNER

ROCKY GRAZIANO

W.C. HEINZ

THOM JONES

NORMAN KATKOV

GEORGE PLIMPTON

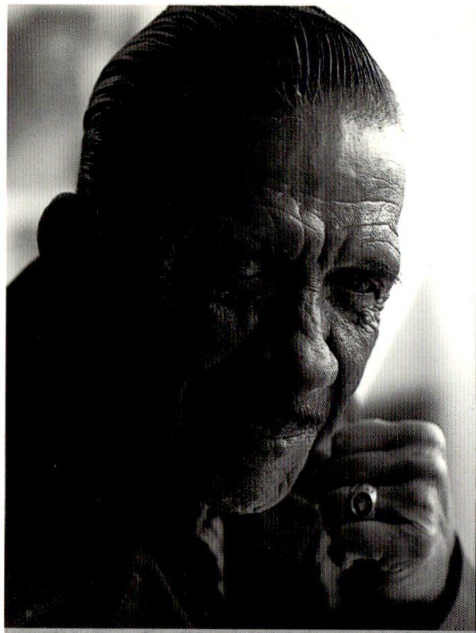
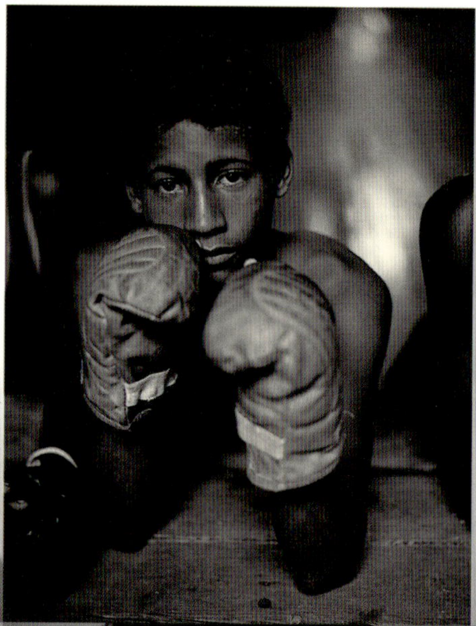
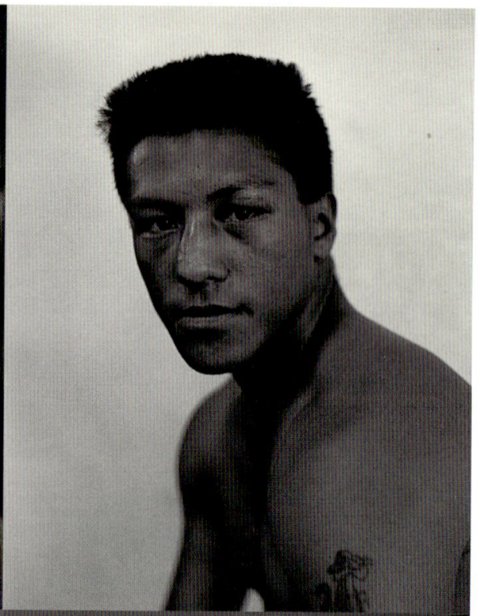
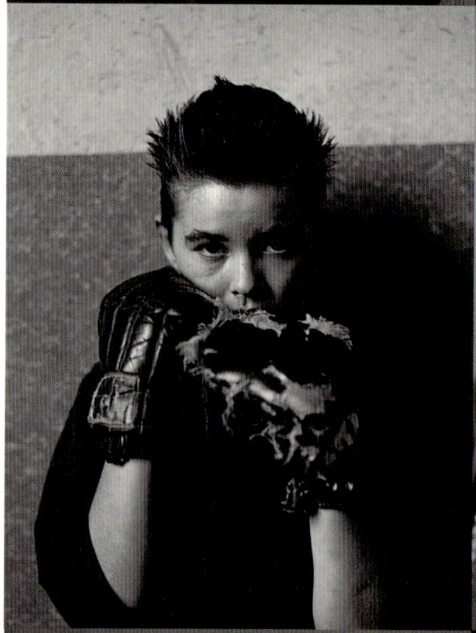
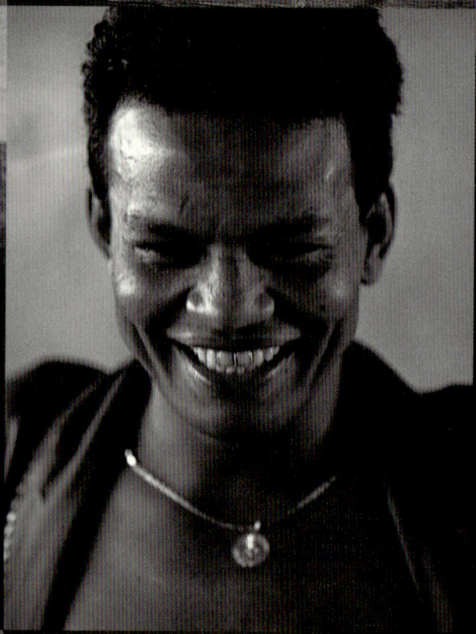
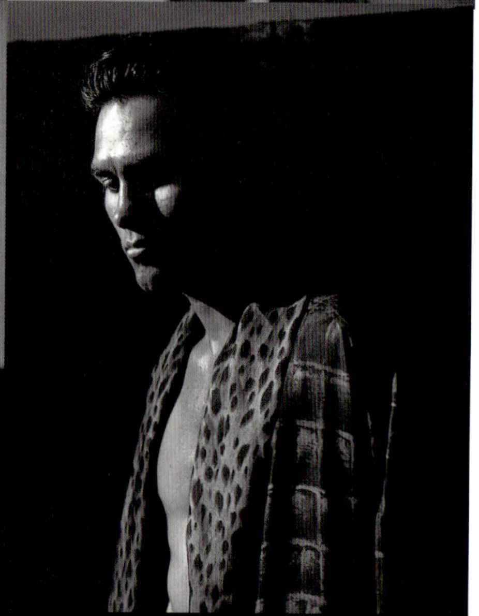
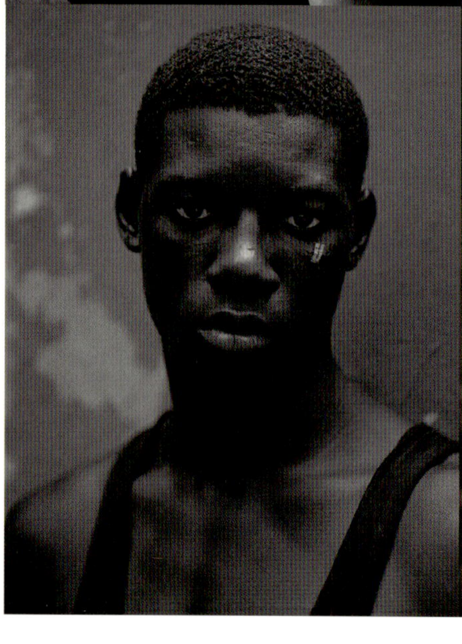
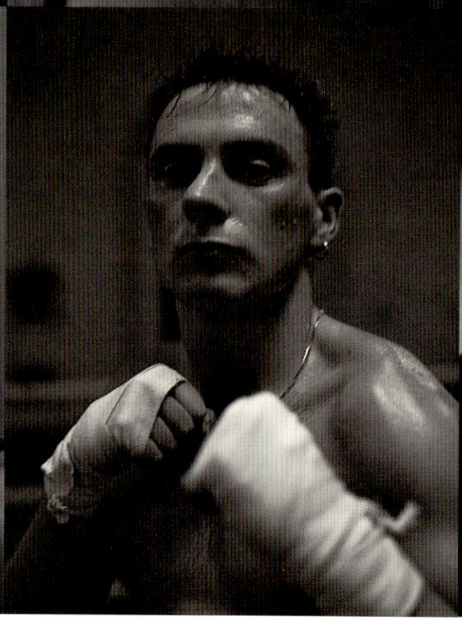
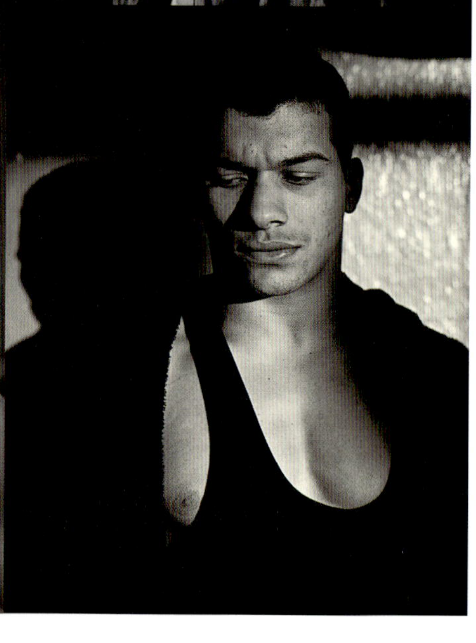

BROOKLYN
NEW YORK
■
MEXICO CITY
MEXICO
■
DUBLIN
IRELAND
■
HAVANA
CUBA

INTRODUCTION
KURT MARKUS

I was maybe ten years old when I fought a fight in a ring. My cousin, four years older than I, talked me into it. He was training in the little gym above the Pastime Bar, on the main street in Whitefish, Montana, where we lived. He said the club needed a body to fill the lightest weight class on the amateur card between our town and the neighboring town, Columbia Falls, which carried an earned reputation that the men, women, and children who lived there were pound-for-pound tougher than we were. I was going to lose. That much seemed a given. But I said, yes, I'd fight because my cousin was my hero.

In the locker room the night of the fight, I struggled with the club's smallest trunks, which swam over my midsection from well below my knees nearly up to my chest. Not only was I about to be bloodied, I had the added indignity of not looking like a fighter even before the beginning bell. I can recall my emotions, and the smells of the gym, the weight of the huge gloves on my tiny fists, the coldness of the stool in my corner—all those very real and immediate facts—as if I had fought that three-rounder only moments ago. It may be my most enduring and vivid recollection of my youth. Whatever else I did until high school is all vagueness; boxing, because it is as much about preparation and anticipation as it is the event itself, stretches time, turns it into a special effect.

I did lose. No one but me, and the other boy, will remember. I wonder now who will remember the boxers on these pages thirty years from today. Probably not many. Because they don't have names like Dempsey, Robinson, or Ali, they have been caught by the camera in a place like Purgatory, a time between winning and losing. They are, in a way, not even fighters because they are not fighting. Stripped, vulnerable, they show their greatness. Am I reading too much into them? Is there not something in them that wants to be in all of us?

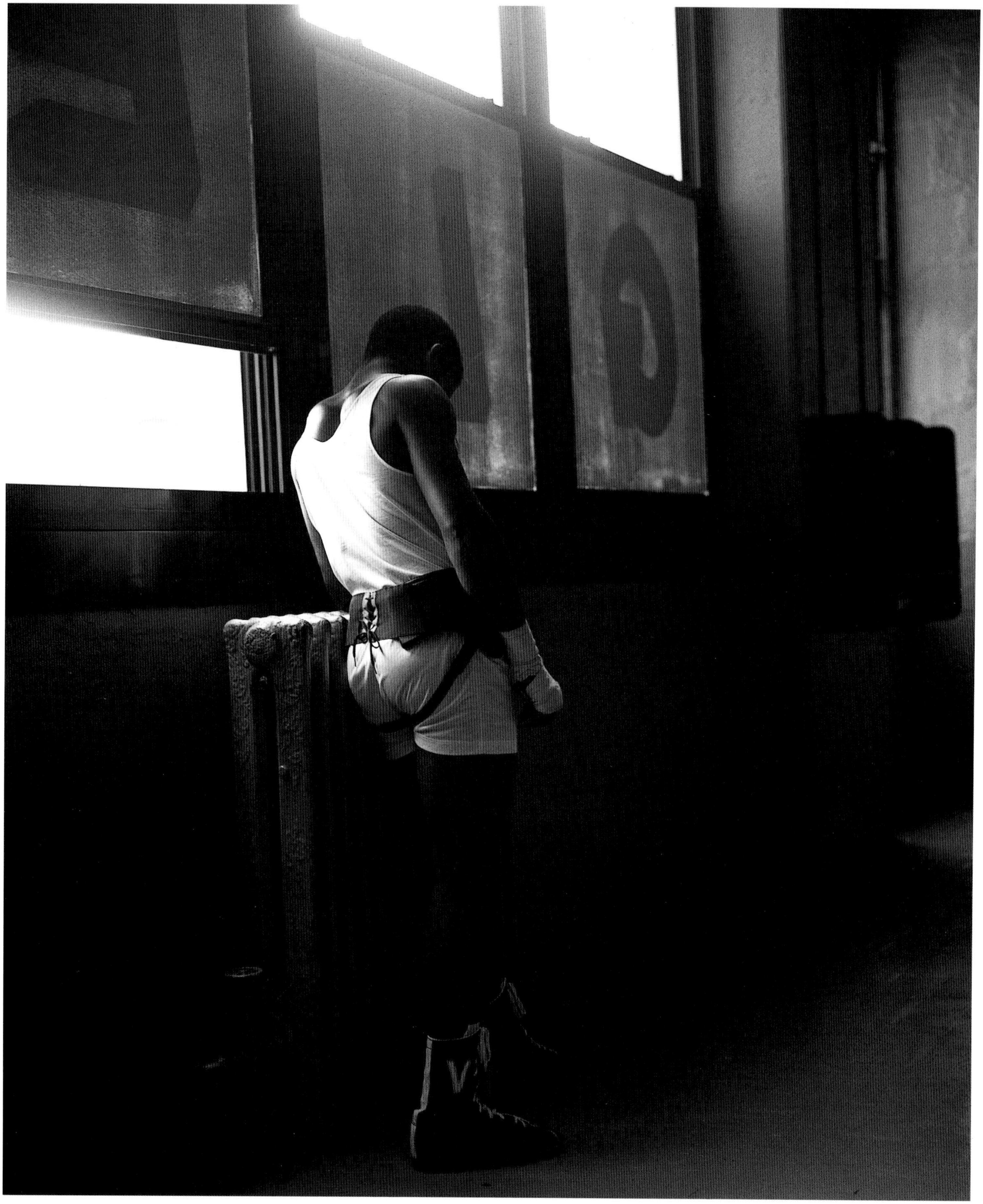

BROOKLYN
NEW YORK, OCTOBER 1990

It's been seven years since I photographed these boxers in Gleason's Gym, so I don't have those immediate impressions to draw on, and I'm stuck to put myself back in the second-floor gym just off the Brooklyn Bridge, away from Manhattan where you think it should be, in an industrial section of the borough, and remember.

That I was in Gleason's at all was the doing of Maria, my wife and my partner in picture making, and it was her early enthusiasm that got me going. Boxing wasn't a scene that I knew. And I wasn't sure boxing was ready for fashion. Because the point of the shoot was to be fashion, to fill a few pages in *Esquire,* I was mindful that there would be some necessary handling of the fighters, and maybe these fighters wouldn't take to that handling, thank you very much. Who could blame them?

As it worked out, the most dangerous leg of our two-day shoot was the first day's drive to the gym, when our van driver, Vinnie, got broadsided by a cab in Manhattan traffic. When Vinnie got out to examine the damage, he heatedly confronted a nervous, non-English speaking cabby fresh from Turkey. The fighters at Gleason's, by comparison, were gentlemen to a man.

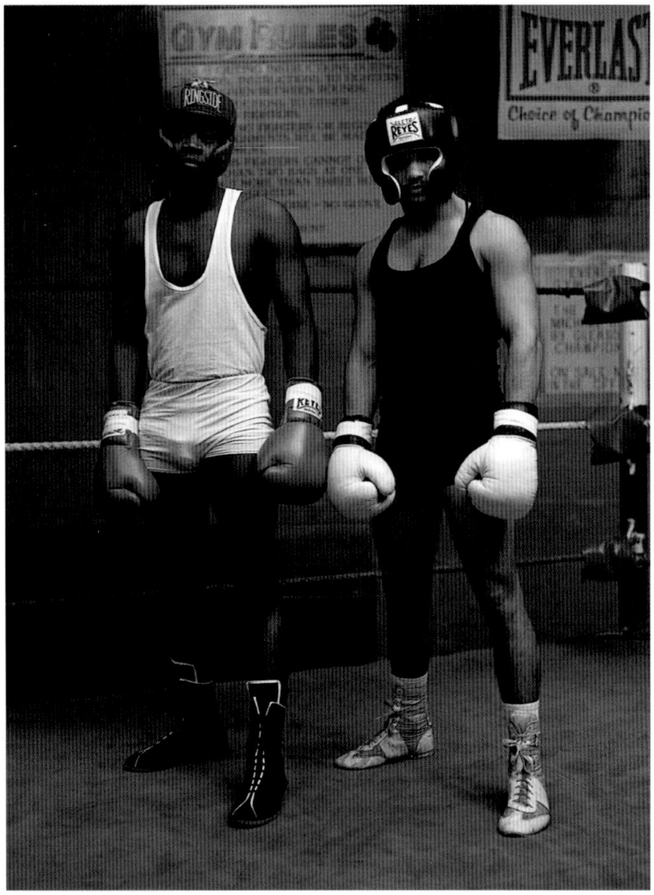
GYM RULES
EVERLAST
RINGSIDE
REYES

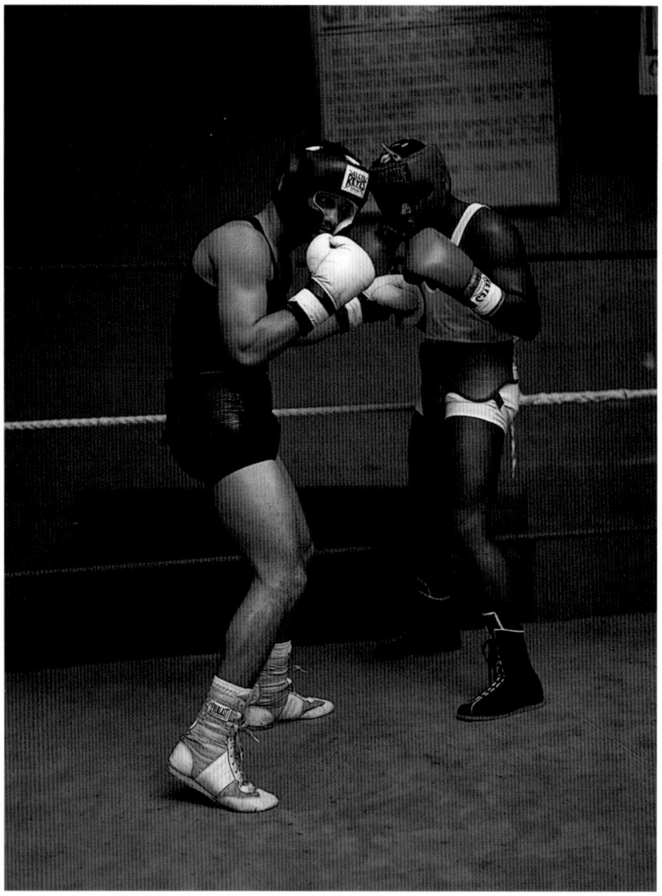
REYES

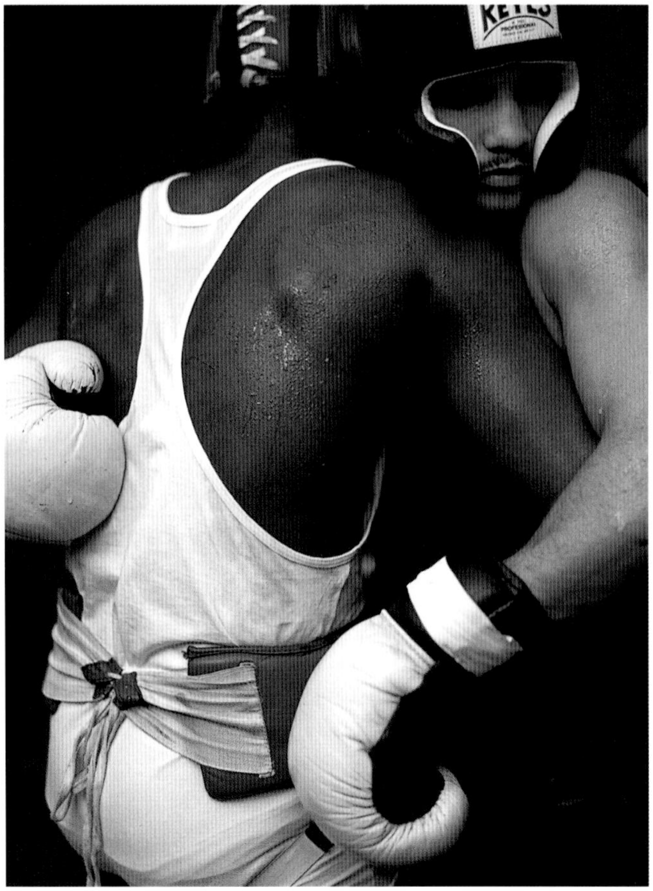
REYES

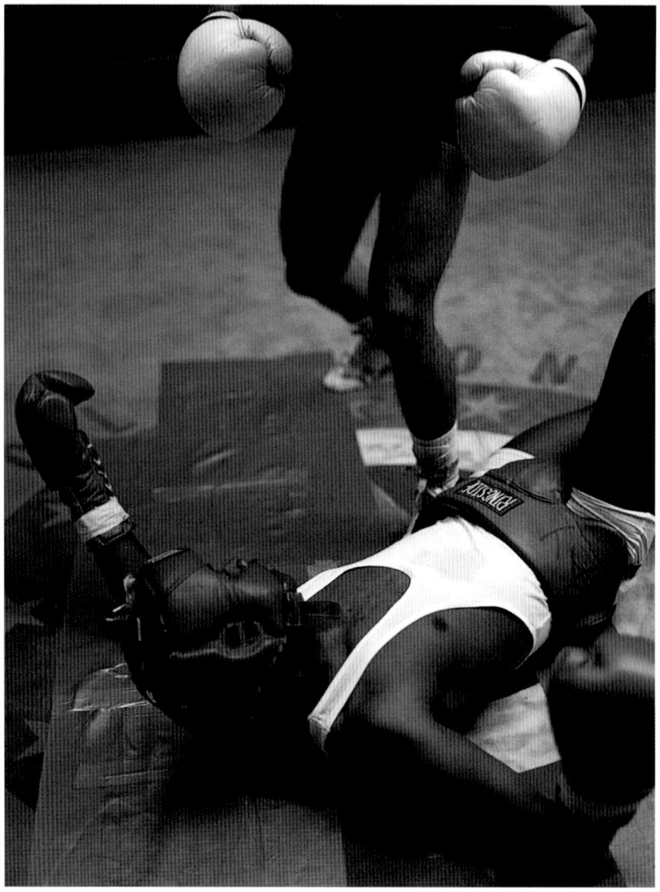
RINGSIDE

It's not difficult to notice how boxing—at least the kind practiced at Gleason's—works to isolate men. There's all this classing going on: weight, ranking, experience, age. I'm sure the thinking here is that everyone wants a fair fight, that nobody should be overmatched, especially in the beginning when their ring skills are raw and untested. But the price of this strict division of labor is a loss of what a member of a team can have, namely the freemasonry that comes with going through a knothole together, *all together*, at the very same moment. The boxers at Gleason's looked to be inside themselves from the time they walked in until the time they showered and left.

Not once have I felt that by doing photographs of boxers I would uncover some truth about the sport. Nor have I desired to photograph the name fighters of our time. I have done a little celebrity work for the magazines and I learned there is nothing inherently rewarding to it; like anything else in picture making, success depends on the person, the day, the light, a floating or sinking vibe, was there or was there not luck, was there or was there not film in the camera. What I was after when we went to Gleason's was to witness the event which occurs in most men's lives at least once: the holding up of fists. It's a singular gesture, and rarely do you see women do it, even now. If you're born male, by the time you're a high school graduate you've most likely either received a bare-fisted shot to the face, or dealt one.

You know the sickening sound of bone whacking bone. You know, too, that if the fight wasn't yours you damned sure wanted to be prepared for the one that would be. And whether you wanted to or not, you suddenly got interested in boxing.

I have, whenever possible, put names to the faces of the fighters in this book. Through no intention of my own there may be a few names fight fans will recognize. What started in Gleason's and ended in Havana was not the further cataloging and isolating of boxers by their given names or monikers but the search for what might exist in every man. Perhaps here, in this book, boxers are of a family not so unfamiliar to you and me. Just take a good wide stance and raise your fists and tell me, how does it feel?

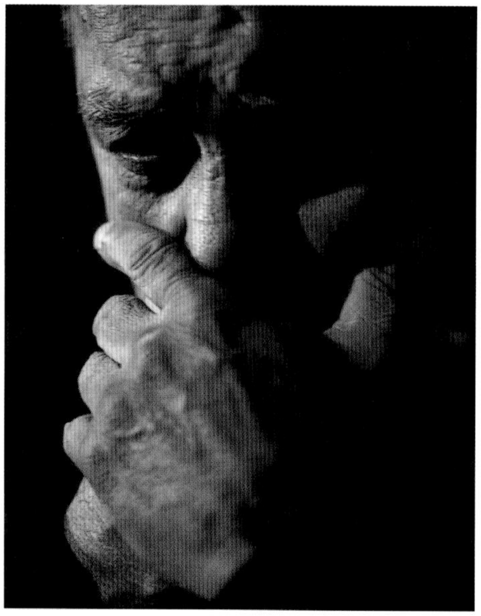

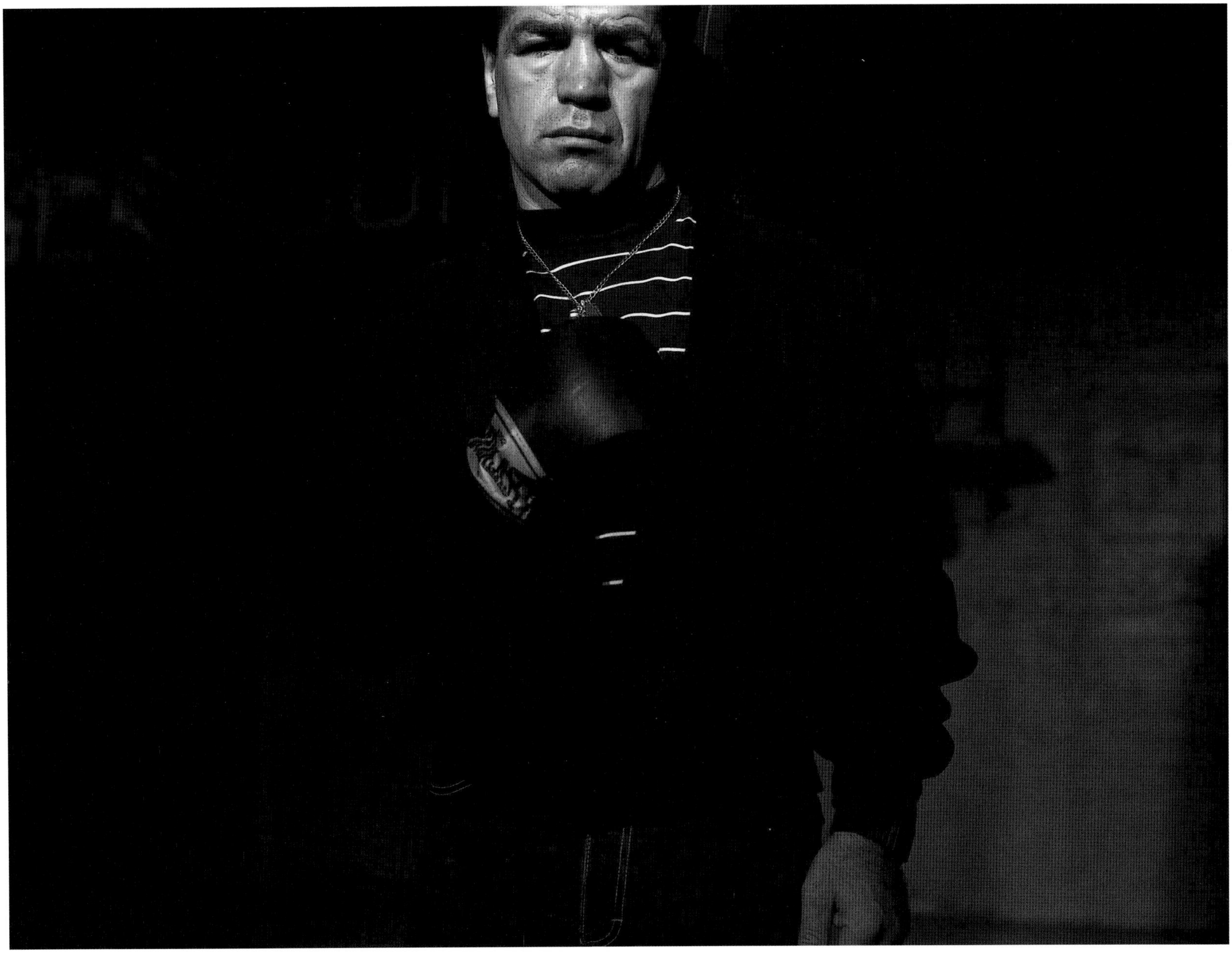

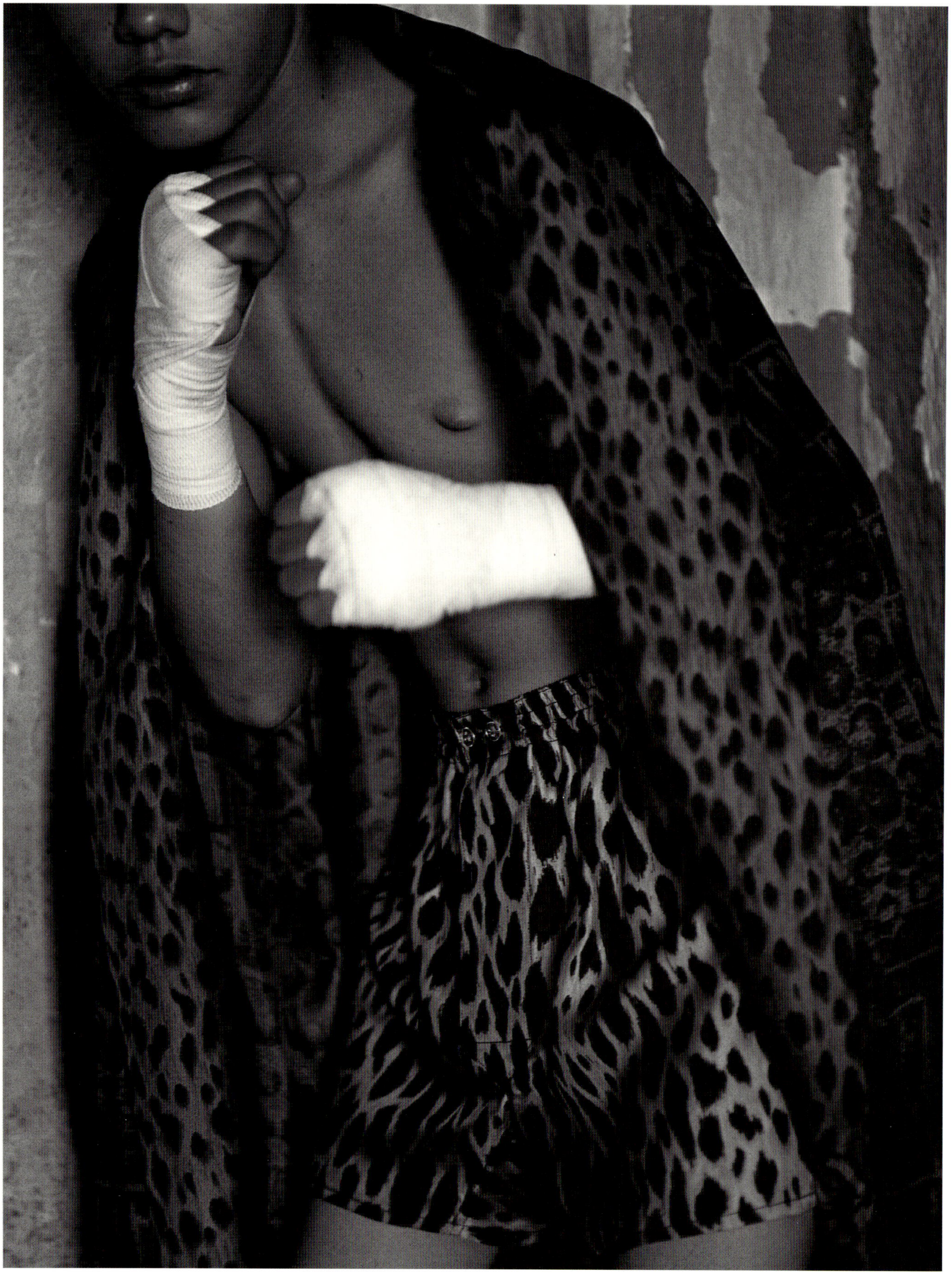

MEXICO CITY

MEXICO, FEBRUARY 1992

These are photographs commissioned for a fashion story, and therefore you should look them over with a great deal of suspicion. The fighters shown here may have been made over, altered, touched, changed. The clothes they wear, excepting personalized trunks, may not be their own. Many fighters got haircuts. How they looked before we walked into the gym may bear small resemblance to what you see here.

This statement of fact, this unmasking, is written by a photographer who would, if left to his own vision, leave people pretty much alone. That is, I am happiest when I haven't had anything to do with what the subject looks like, preferring to believe our individuality is actually quite sacred, that to tamper with a person's identity is dangerous. Live and let live often works to create a photograph with staying power, meaning that when you encounter it again, it not only contains its original magic, but new truths emerge which can make you happy one more time.

I not only threw that thinking away when I set out to do boxing photographs in 1990, I pitched it without reservation. These photographs which I, producer-stylist Maria Markus and hairdresser-stylist Eric Gabriel collaborated on are somehow made better, I think, by the intervention: i.e., what you see is what you get, but maybe there's a light or two thrown onto the shadowy realm of spirit, the way boxing feels, the particular manner in which a fighter's eyes reflect a world. Boxers require idealization, it seems to me, to be accurately portrayed, unlike, say, celebrities who jump off the page when they are the most themselves, the least fussed with, styled, made-up, or conceptualized. I laugh at myself for saying this, but boxers look the way they ought to, somehow, when they have been made victims of fashion.

So what were the boxers like? On the outside, as you can see for yourself in the photographs, they are wonderfully conditioned, their bodies truly their instruments, no more muscle than necessary, no less, either. Theirs is an anatomy of function. They train the body to do what they ask, and the beauty of it is in the

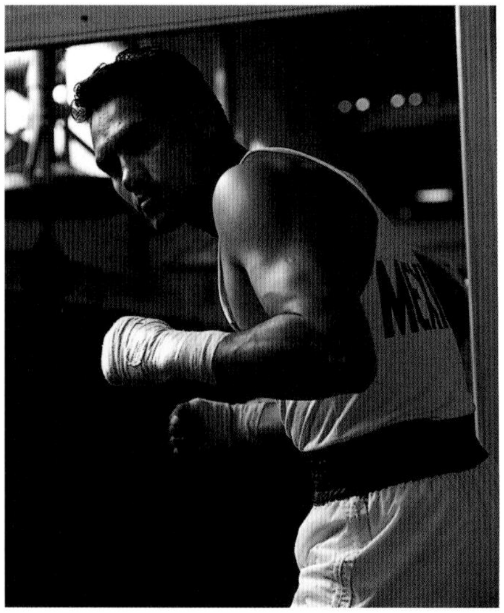

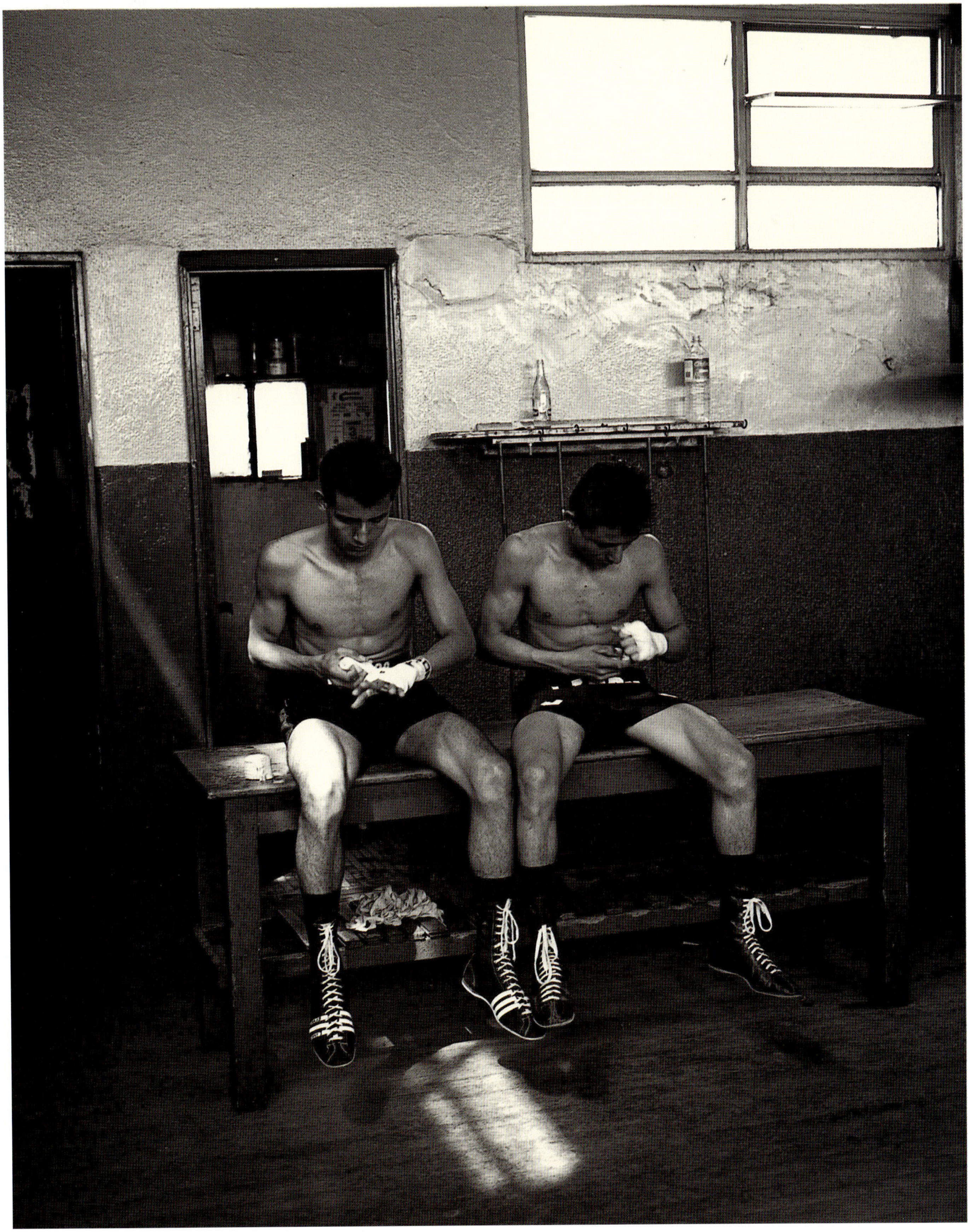

performance—perhaps this is a reason they seem at ease within themselves. Standing, flat-footed, they are not particularly imposing, nor do they immediately cause you to keep your distance. Because they are accustomed to having their body space violated, violently, they are supremely approachable; it is nothing to them that you walk up and adjust a robe or lay a hand on them in order to move them to a specific spot. I was surprised to find them loose to the touch, almost malleable.

I came to believe we could do anything we wished to these fighters. There was not much left to do to, come to think of it, short of asking them to wear nothing. Not everyone can appear in public in just their underwear and not have doubts. Most fighters, we learned, may carry doubts, but not about what to wear. I, too, stopped noticing what they had on, and lost myself in them.

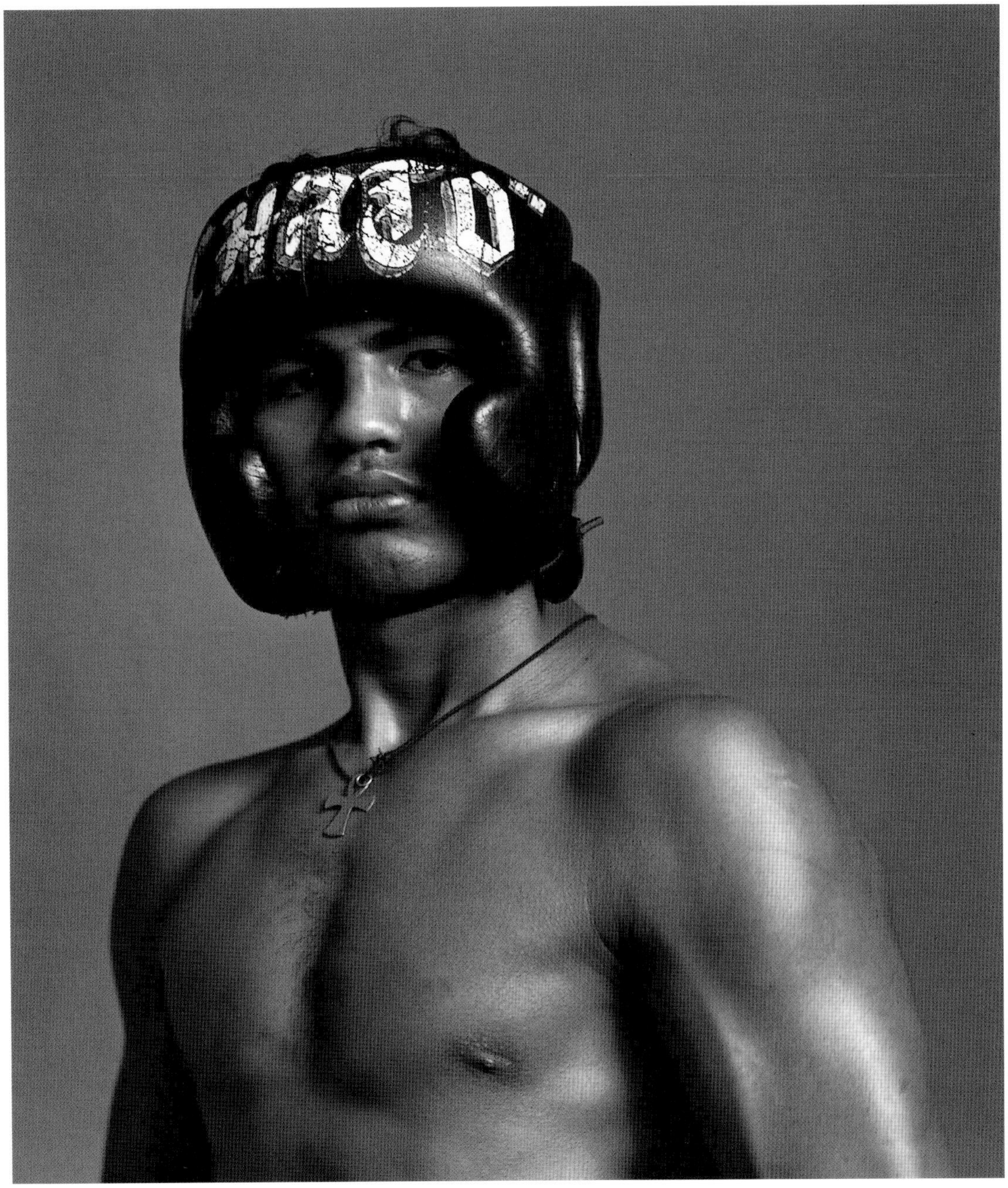

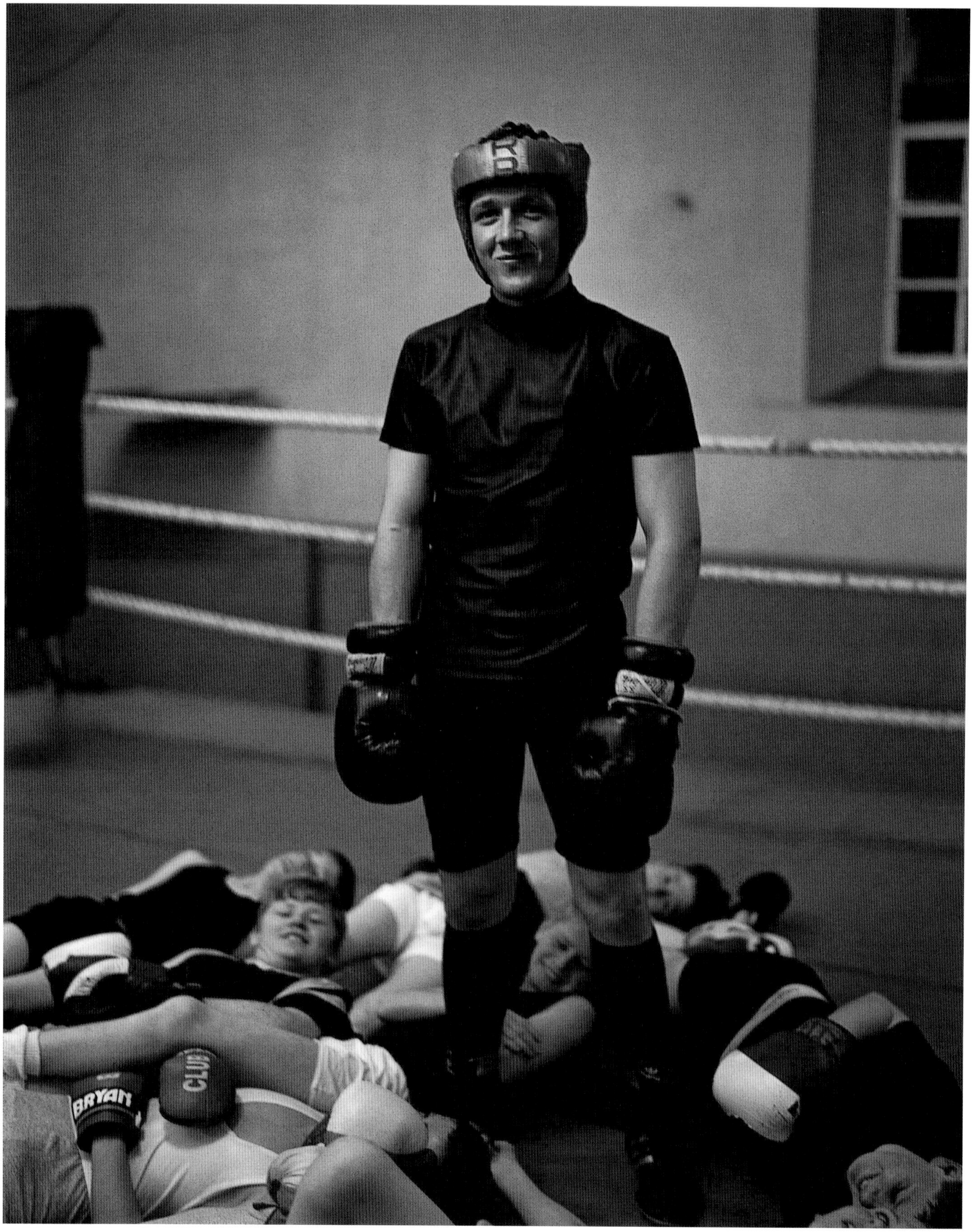
BRYAN

DUBLIN

IRELAND, OCTOBER 1992

These are the faces I imagined I'd see someday, but I never imagined I'd see so many. And these are but a few of the hundreds of boxers filling the small clubs scattered throughout Dublin and other major Irish cities.

They are clean faces, mostly. Straight, unbroken noses. Regular ears. Eyes lit up, hopeful. Normal boys and young men. Because there is no professional boxing in Ireland, boxing has retained much of its innocence, and transparency, and it has left little scarring in its path.

Laughter, both the deep and slow kind from the heavies, and the downy and quick sort from the young, runs through the worn gymnasiums as free as the comings and goings of

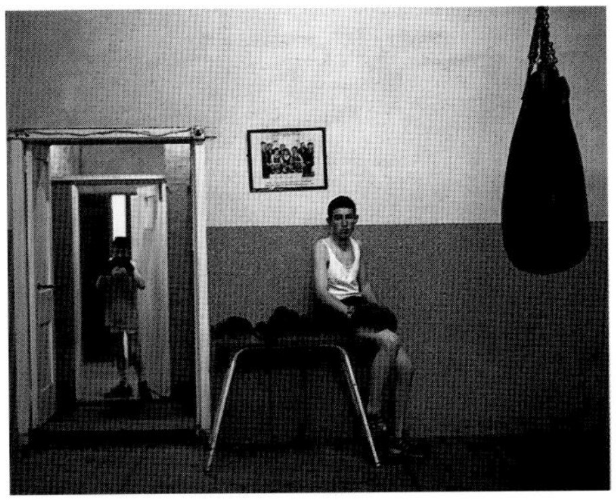

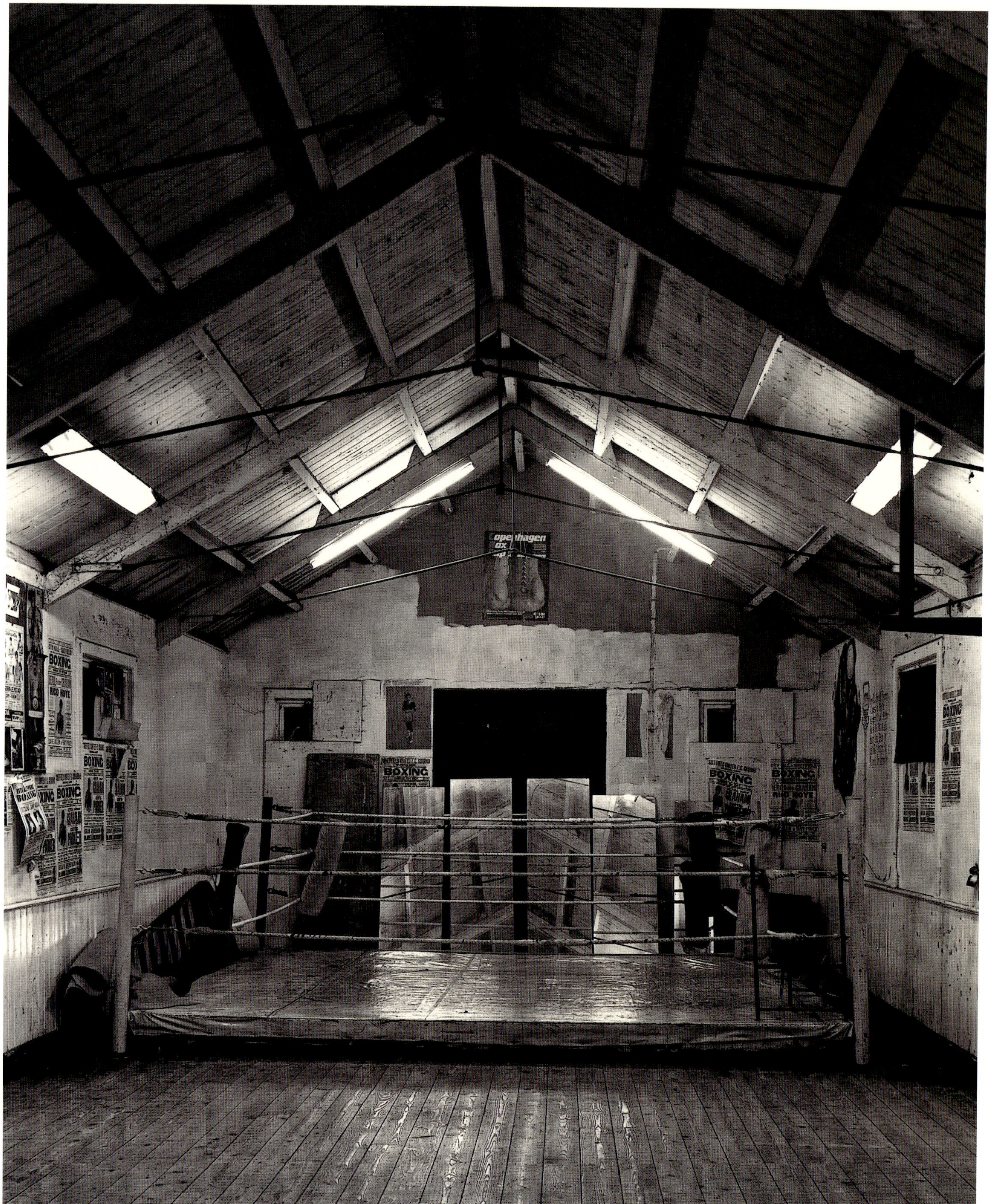
Copenhagen
BOXING
RICO HOYE

sparrows. Laughter. Giggles. The sounds of leather slapping leather, leather weighing into weighted canvas, leather thudding emptily into flesh. Bells, dings, and gongs. Rope, feet tapping, tap, tap, tapping. Words with exclamation points. Jab! Break! Maleness against maleness, hitting, maleness holding maleness, clinching. Laughter. Laughter, how it beautifies the shabby, roped-in square of refereed violence.

It is not what you expect from boxing. What you expect is the desperation of street-toughs with nothing to lose and nowhere to go but up. No joy, certainly, and maybe not much kindness. But because there are boys about, Irish boxing has held on to a grace and humanity that redeems the sport.

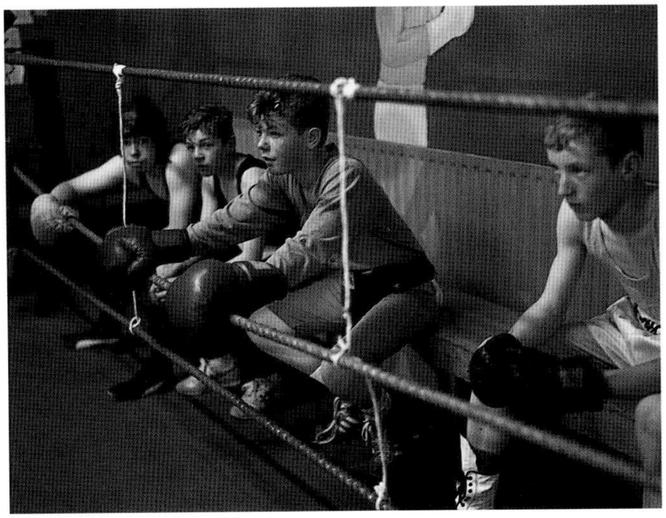

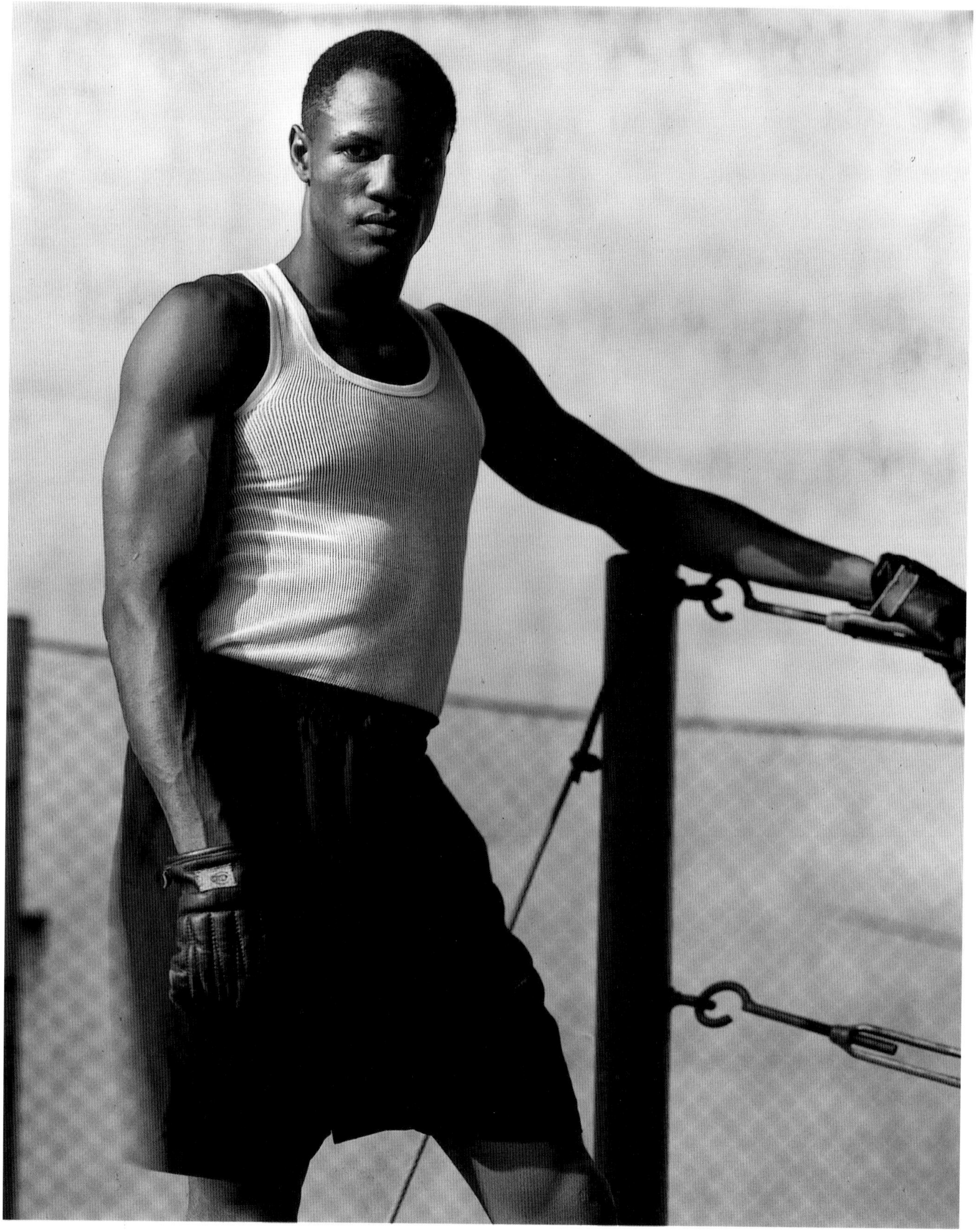

HAVANA
CUBA, OCTOBER 1993

Several kilometers from the city of Havana there is a compound, a finca, where the Cuban boxers are trained. Because concrete is in short supply in today's Cuba, you can tell the Cubans love their boxers because a new training gym is nearly completed, and under construction are new buildings to house the fighters. Meanwhile, the boxers train and spar in one of two small cinderblock rectangles—the ceiling is so low in the primary gym that the club's leading heavyweight and tallest athlete, Felix Savon, has but a few inches of head room—and live dormitory-style in tiny rooms in the center of the finca. An oval running track defines the perimeter. A cookhouse abuts the main gym. At the entrance is a triangular-peaked guard shack which is manned by an old man with a carbine and an underfed dog of unknown breed. I saw a couple domestic-sized air conditioners here and there, but between the frequent electrical black-outs that occur without warning and the unrelenting humidity and heat, there was no cooling refuge for the world's finest amateur boxers.

After watching the Cubans train a couple days, I didn't need creative thought to know why they're good: they're disciplined, and they sweat. A lot. A few minutes of skipping rope or punching the speed bag or sparring in the ring and the boxers have soaked through their trunks and are dripping wet. Some of the young men fight and train in their bare feet, and sometimes they fall down, so slippery do the mats become.

It is difficult to find the words to describe Cuban boxers or the island itself for that matter, the one blending into the other at every seam. After having seen quite a number of boxers in New York, Mexico City, and Dublin, I thought the Cubans were the prettiest (I am dipping into the vocabulary of Muhammad Ali for this one) and most rationally trained (the coaches seemed almost serene). As a born and raised capitalist I initially found the communal way of life around the finca baffling, but I soon came to appreciate that the aloneness of fighting could be

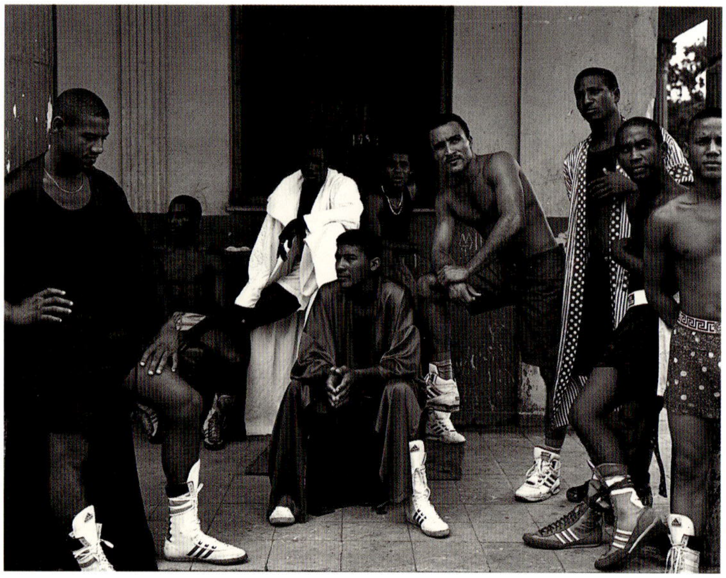

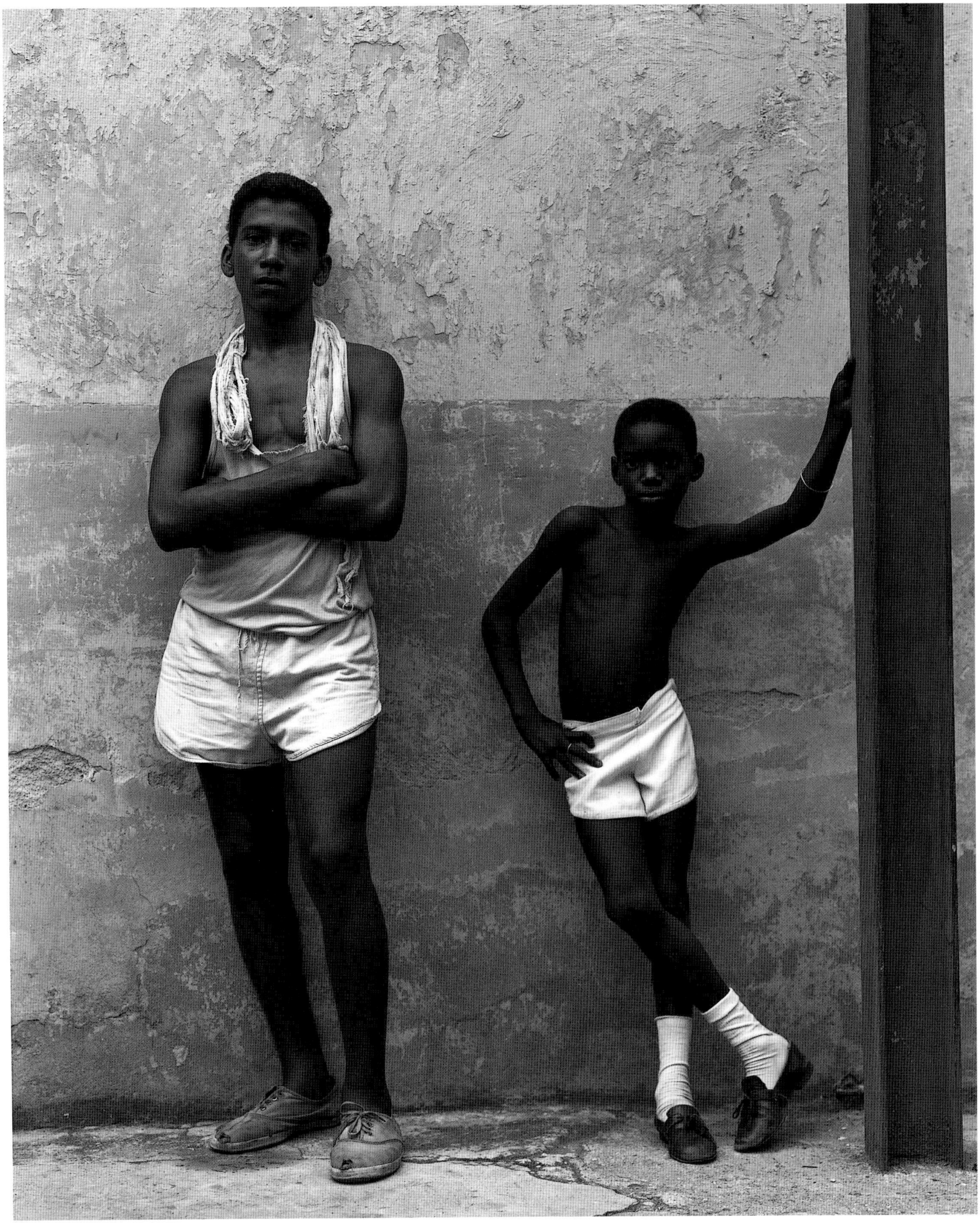

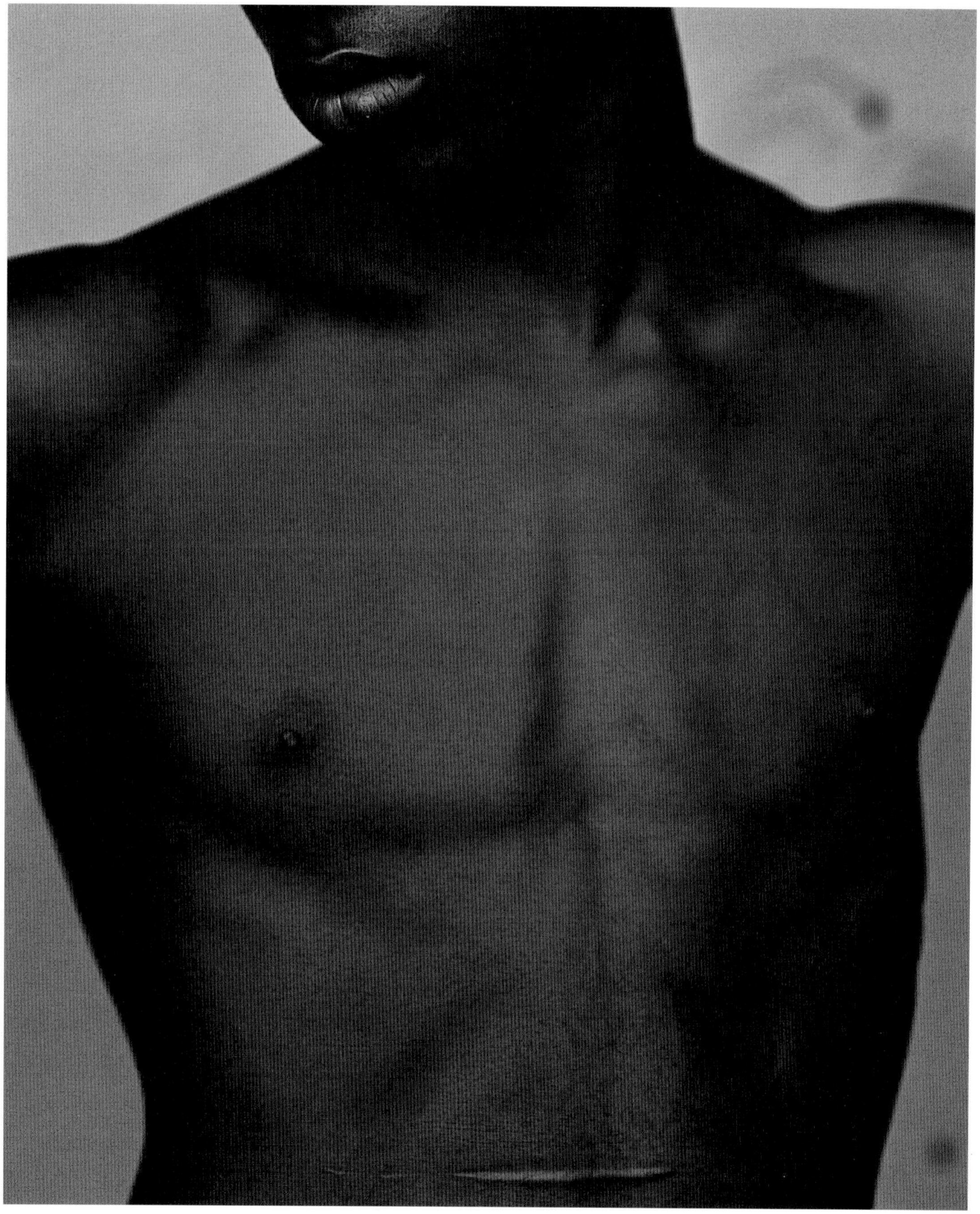

balanced by group support, which seemed in great supply. The chemistry of the team seems more like that of an American college basketball squad, a squad that gets along and relies on the performance of all its members, not just a starring few.

Of course most of the boxers are black, African black, but these Cuban blacks have a grace and ease that only an absence of racism could engender. That there is an outward appearance of harmony between the colors on the streets of Havana is a sign not everything in Fidel's dream for his country has failed. I often felt I was photographing dancers, not boxers, such are the line and tone of these Cuban fighter's bodies, which may help explain why I was so compelled to photograph them as if they were cast in bronze or polished from marble. I see in a boxer's body an ideal of maleness, a body both glorified by severe conditioning and humbled by punishment. Even with clothes on, a conditioned fighter has a nakedness and vulnerability that makes almost any picture a nude.

BOXERS

■

Man, I love boxing. I love everything about it. I love the punches and all the fancy moves. I like sweat and the smell of leather. I love the diet, the training, the structure of each day. I love the individuality, I love the other fighters. I feel privileged to be in their company.

THOM JONES

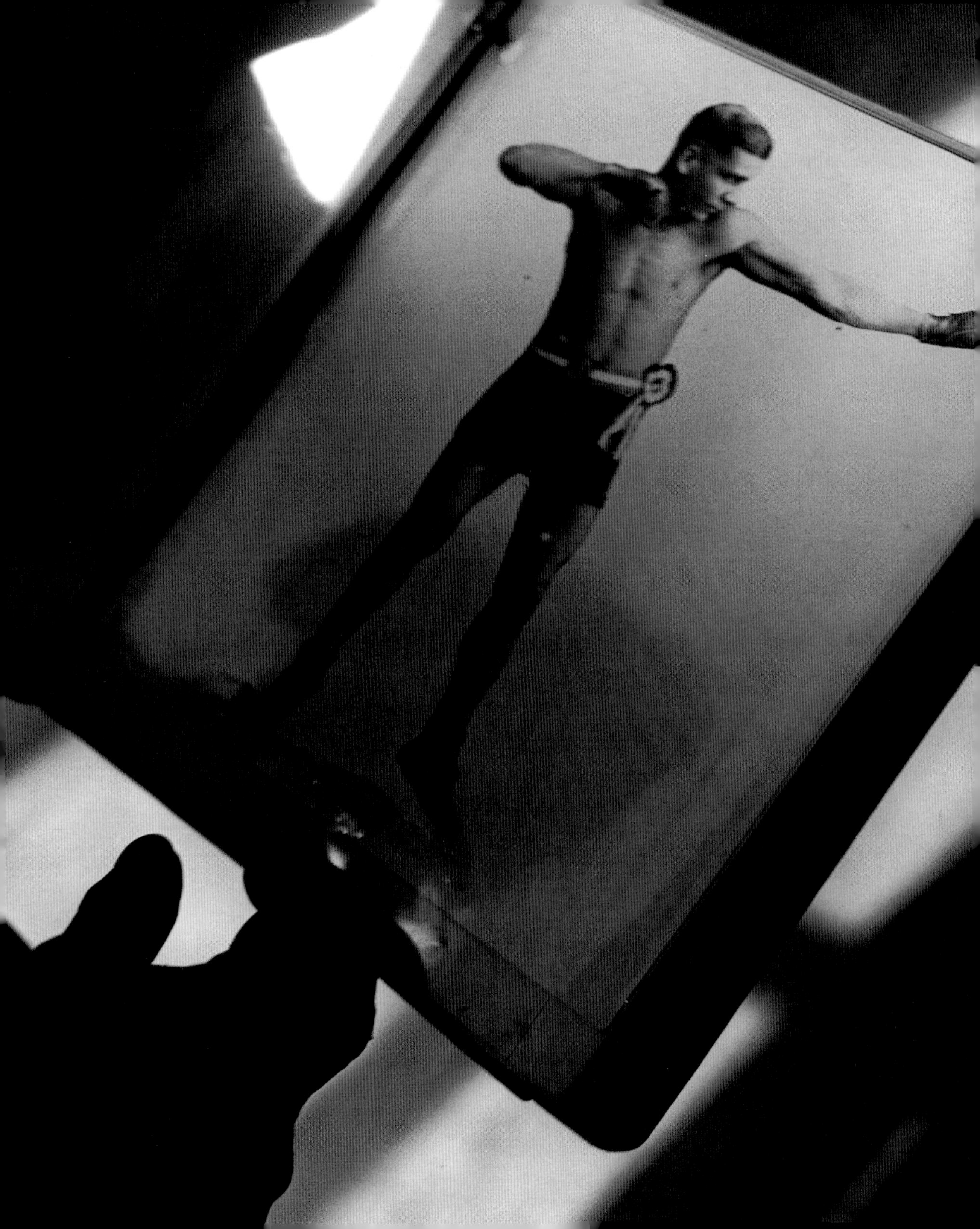

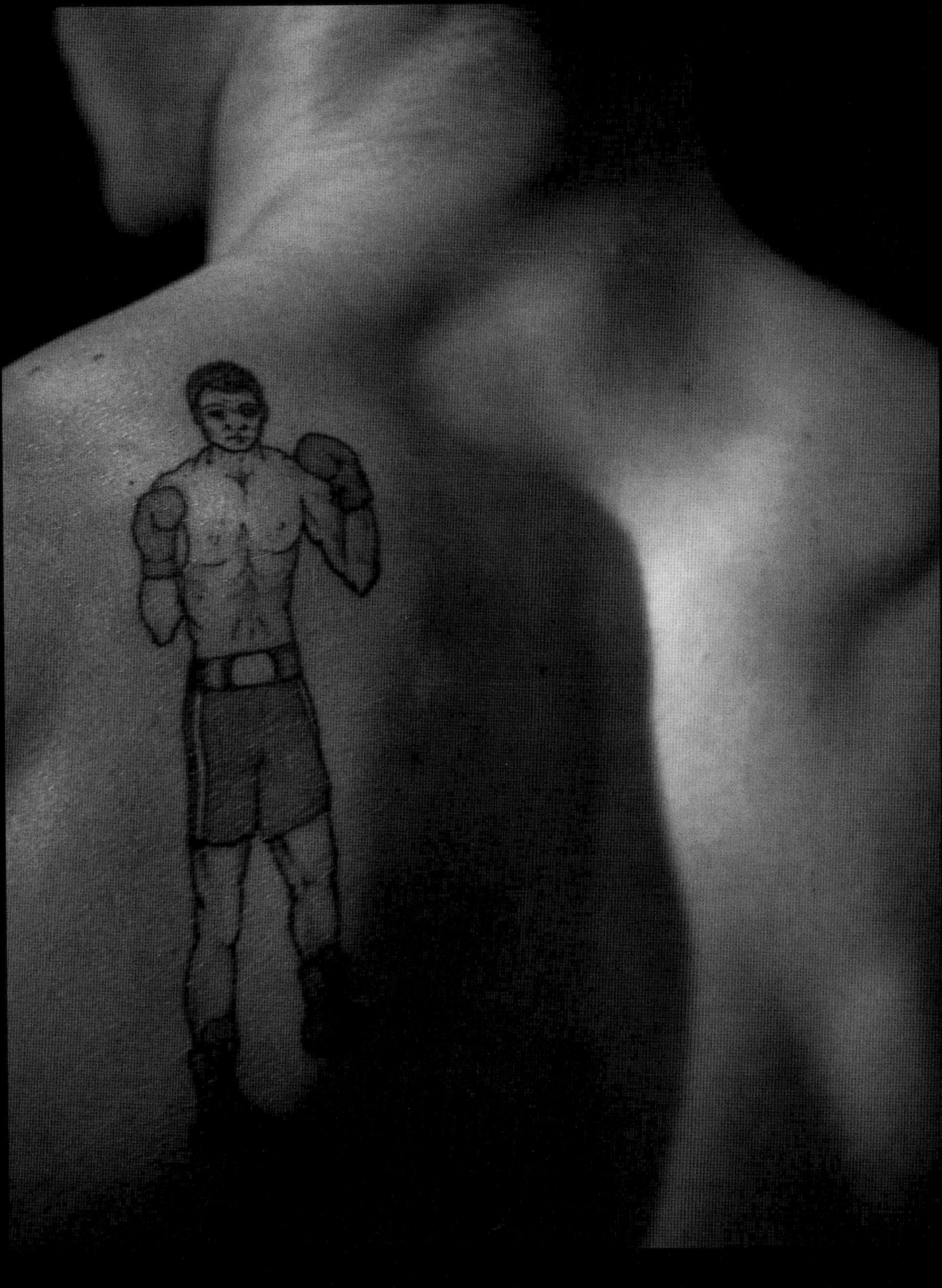

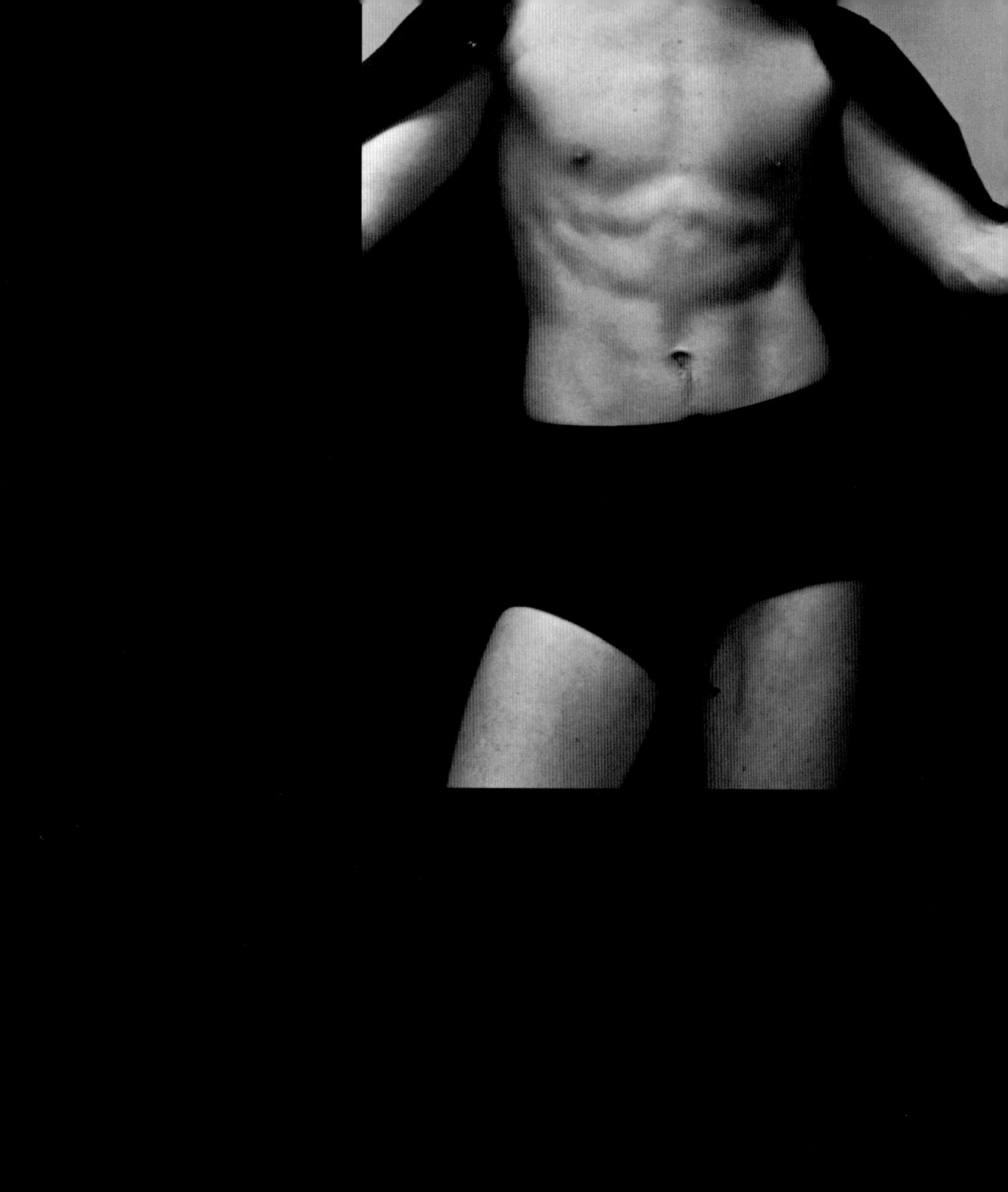

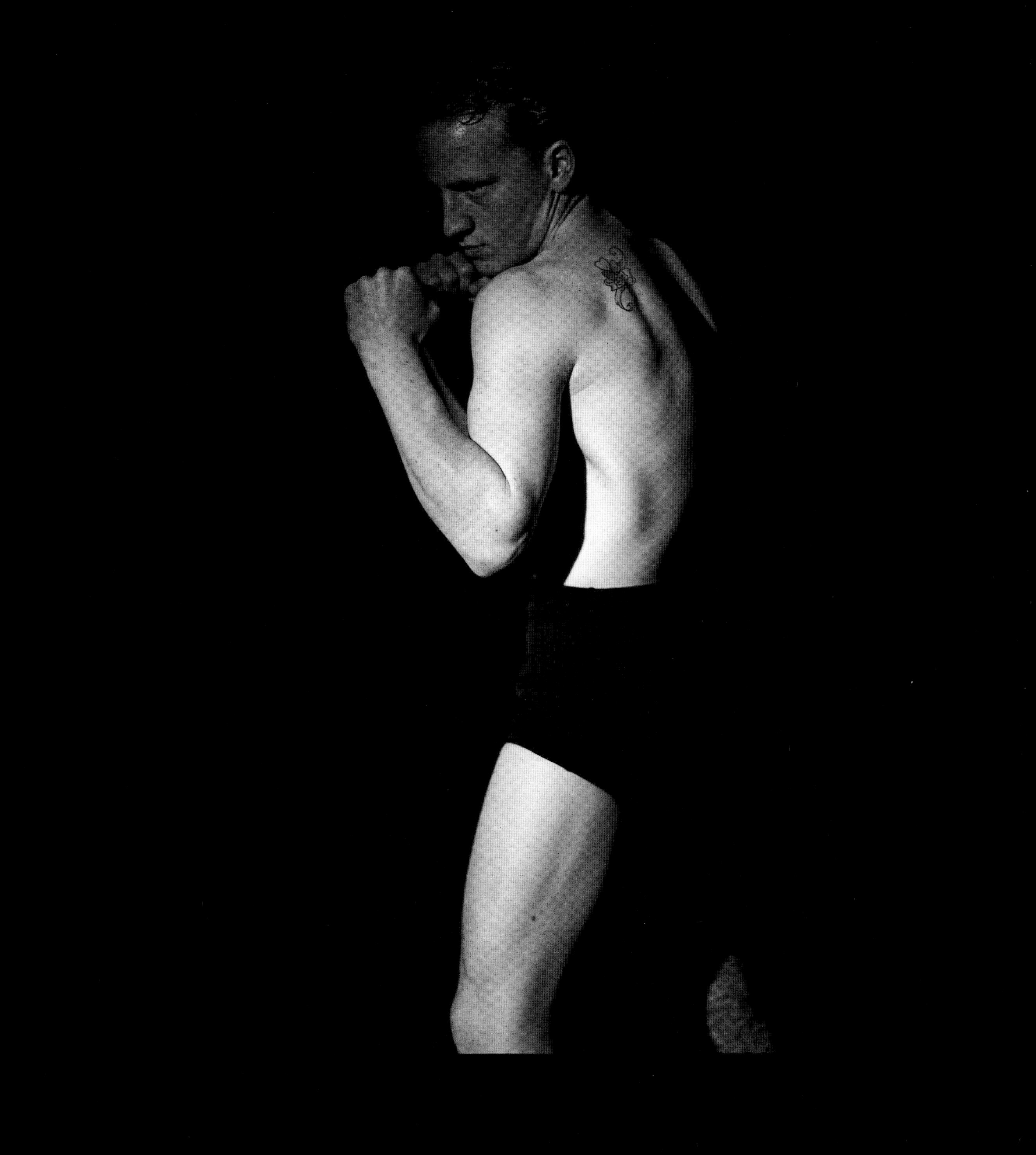

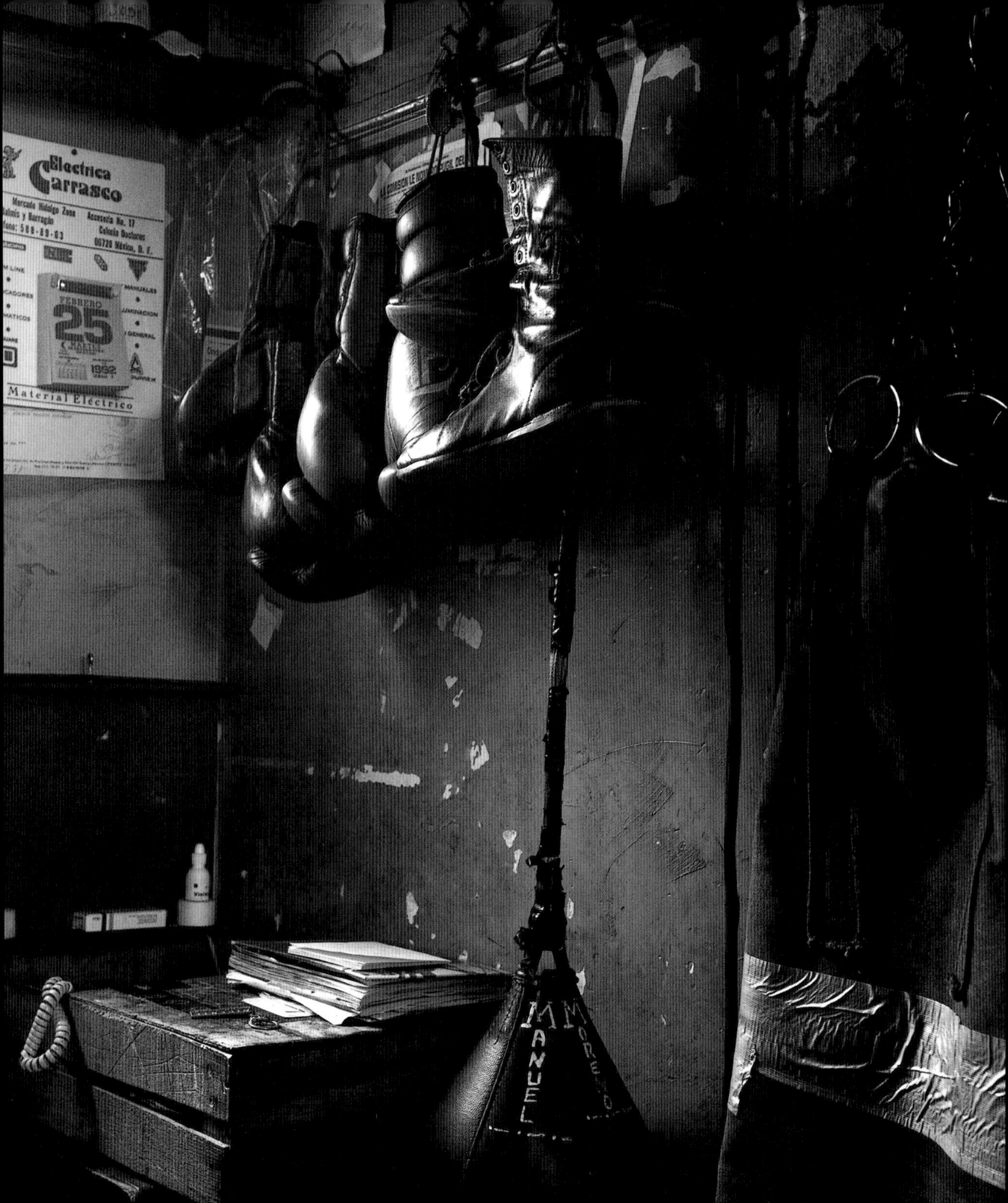
Electrica
Carrasco
FEBRERO
25
1992
Material Eléctrico
MANUEL

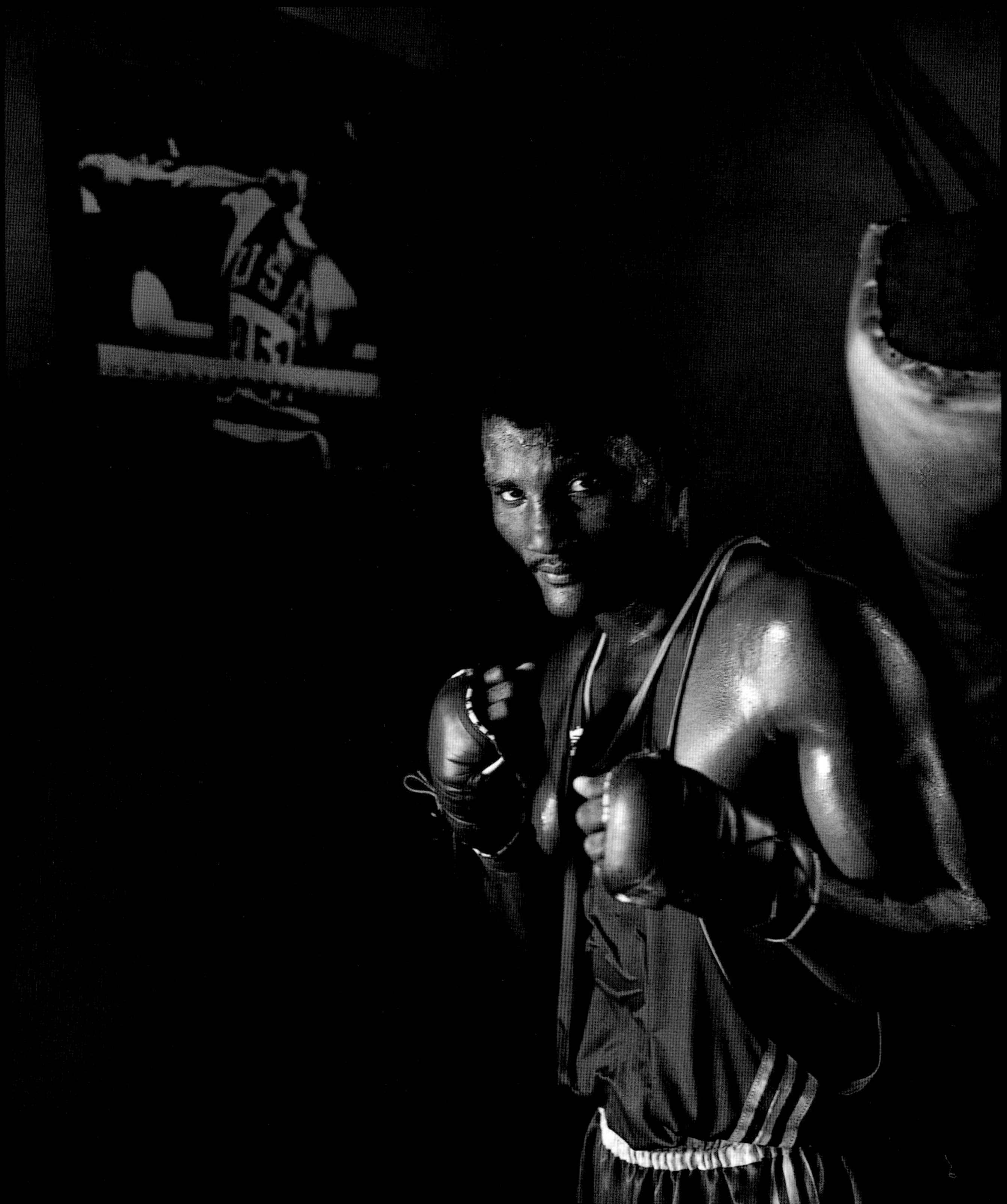
USA

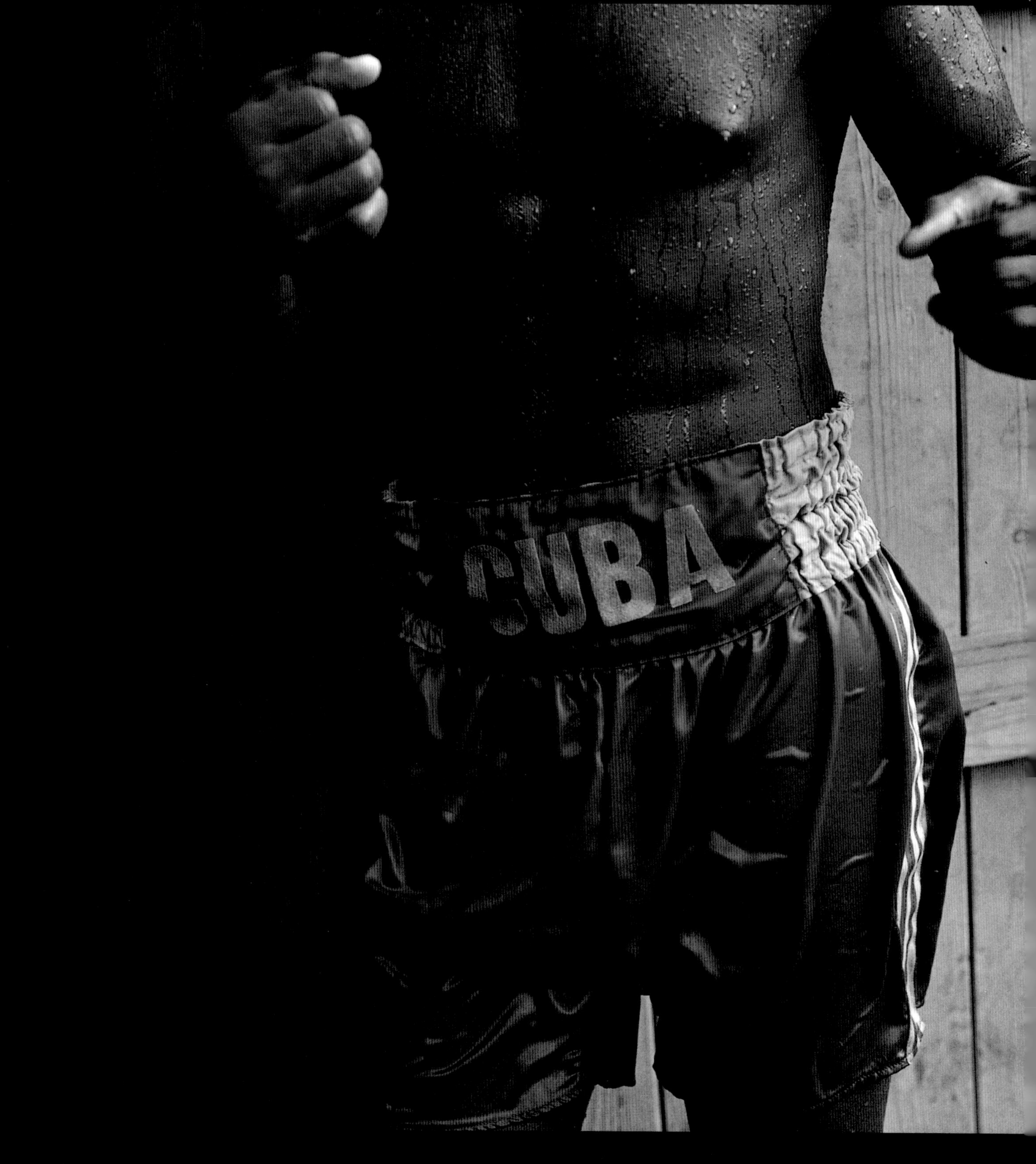
CUBA

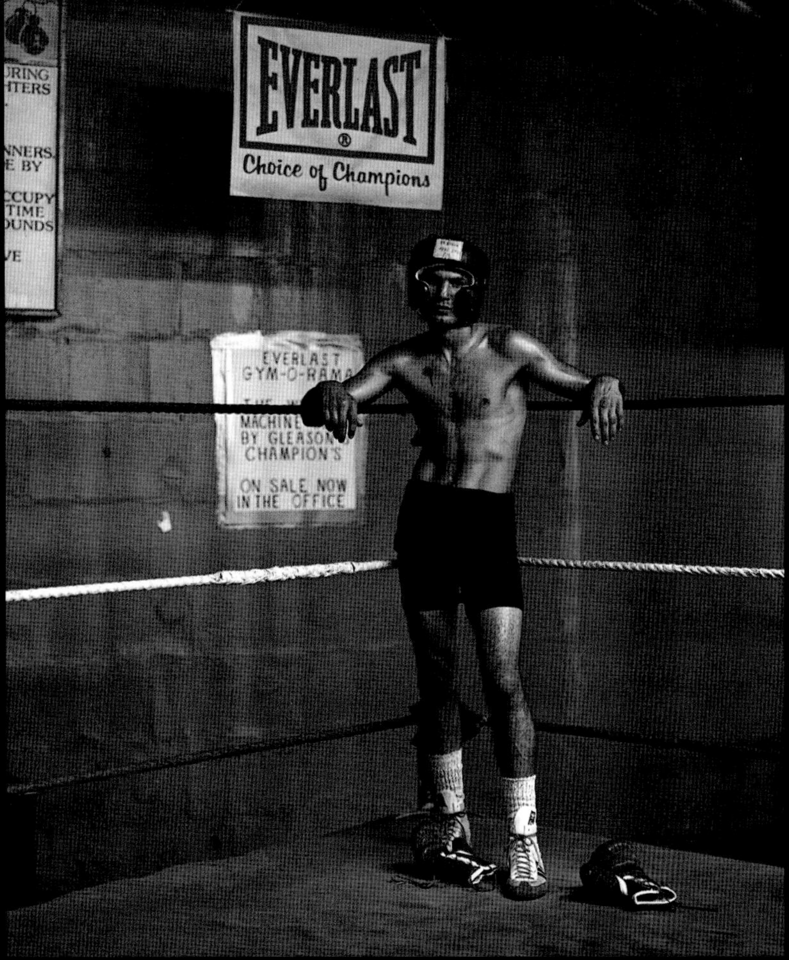
EVERLAST
Choice of Champions
EVERLAST
GYM-O-RAMA
MACHINE
CHAMPION'S
ON SALE NOW
IN THE OFFICE

He turned away and took a step toward the chest of drawers standing at an angle beyond the windows, and knew then why he had come into Young Gino's room. There was the big, double frame that Anna had not bought, which Young Gino had brought home, and in it, the two glossy pictures: the boy on the right and the father on the left.

The boy had dug out Gino's black silk trunks and boxing shoes, and gone to the same photographer across the street from the Rose Room who, twenty years earlier, had taken the father's picture. He had posed the same: right hand high on the bare chest, and left extended; head cocked and shoulders forward.

NORMAN KATKOV

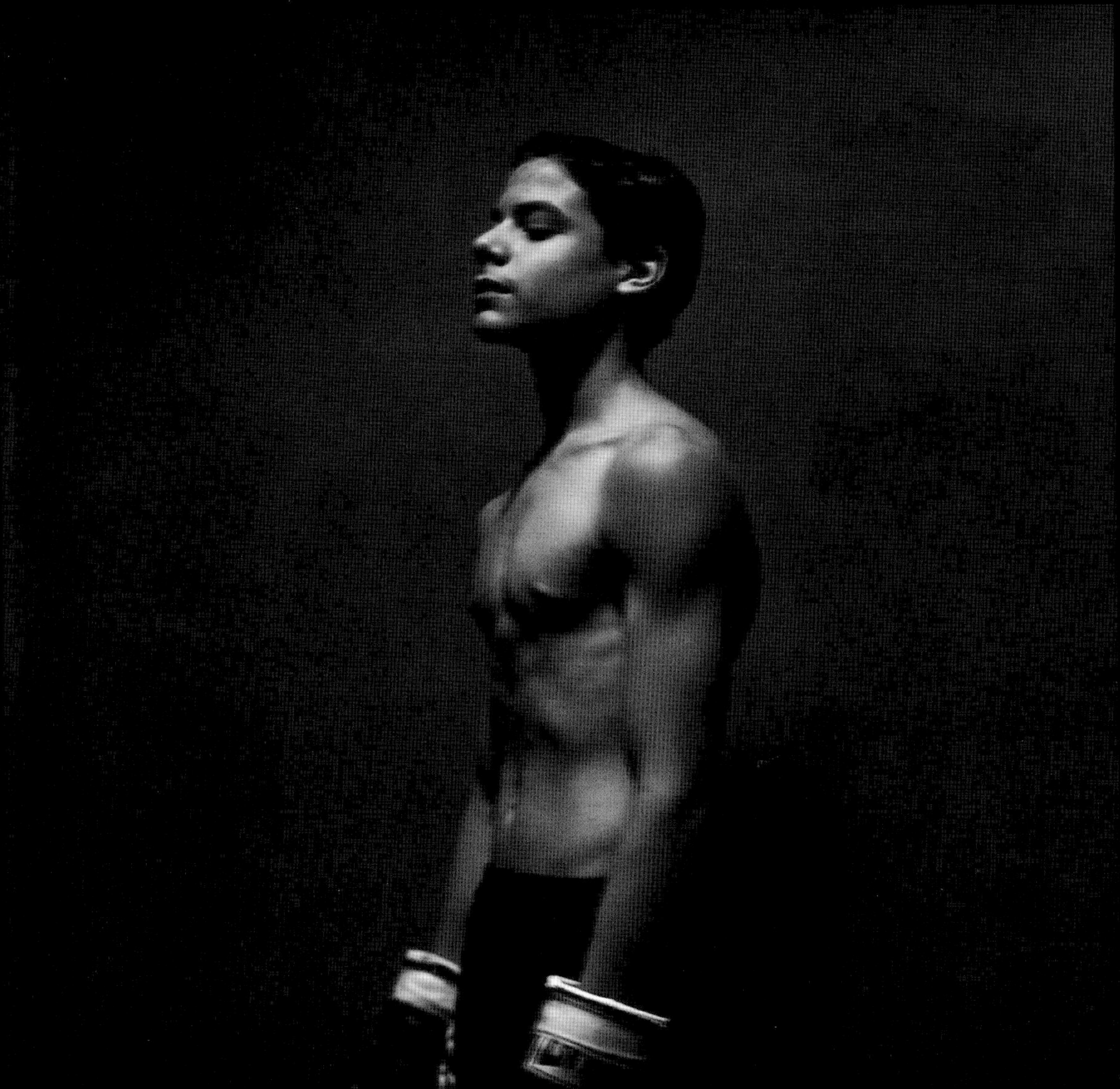

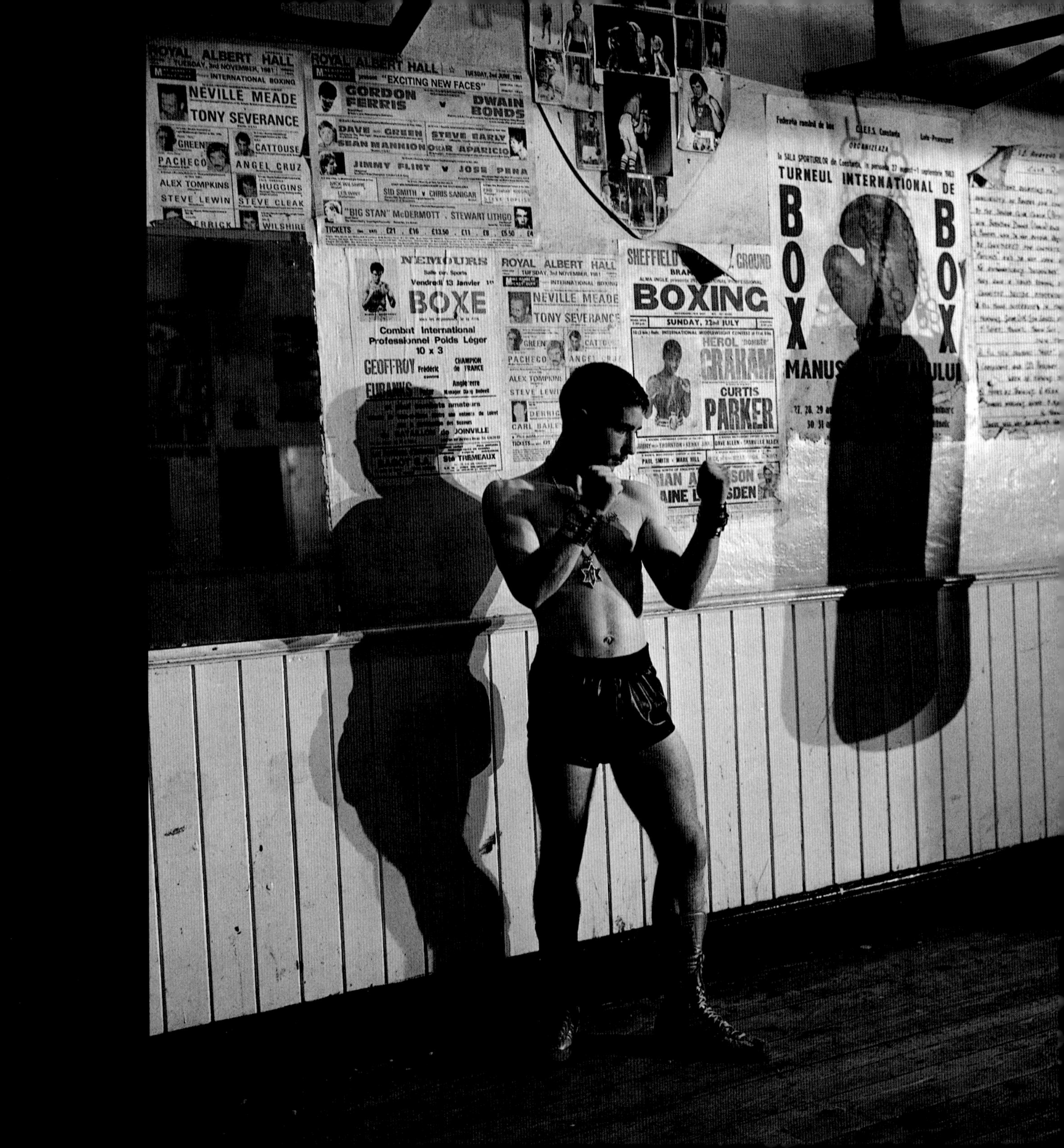
ROYAL ALBERT HALL
TUESDAY, 3rd NOVEMBER, 1981
INTERNATIONAL BOXING
NEVILLE MEADE
TONY SEVERANCE
GREEN
CATTOUSE
PACHECO
ANGEL CRUZ
ALEX TOMPKINS
HUGGINS
STEVE LEWIN
STEVE CLEAK
WILSHIRE
ROYAL ALBERT HALL
"EXCITING NEW FACES"
TUESDAY, 2nd JUNE, 1981
GORDON FERRIS
DWAIN BONDS
DAVE GREEN
STEVE EARLY
SEAN MANNION
OSCAR APARICIO
JIMMY FLINT v JOSE PENA
SID SMITH v CHRIS SANIGAR
"BIG STAN" McDERMOTT
STEWART LITHGO
NEMOURS
Vendredi 13 Janvier
BOXE
Combat International
Professionnel Poids Léger
10 x 3
GEOFFROY
CHAMPION de FRANCE
de JOINVILLE
ROYAL ALBERT HALL
TUESDAY, 3rd NOVEMBER, 1981
INTERNATIONAL BOXING
NEVILLE MEADE
TONY SEVERANCE
GREEN
CATTOUSE
PACHECO
ALEX TOMPKINS
STEVE LEWIN
CARL BAILEY
BOXING
SUNDAY, 22nd JULY
HEROL "BOMBER" GRAHAM
CURTIS PARKER
PAUL SMITH
MARK HILL
TURNEUL INTERNATIONAL DE
BOX
BOX

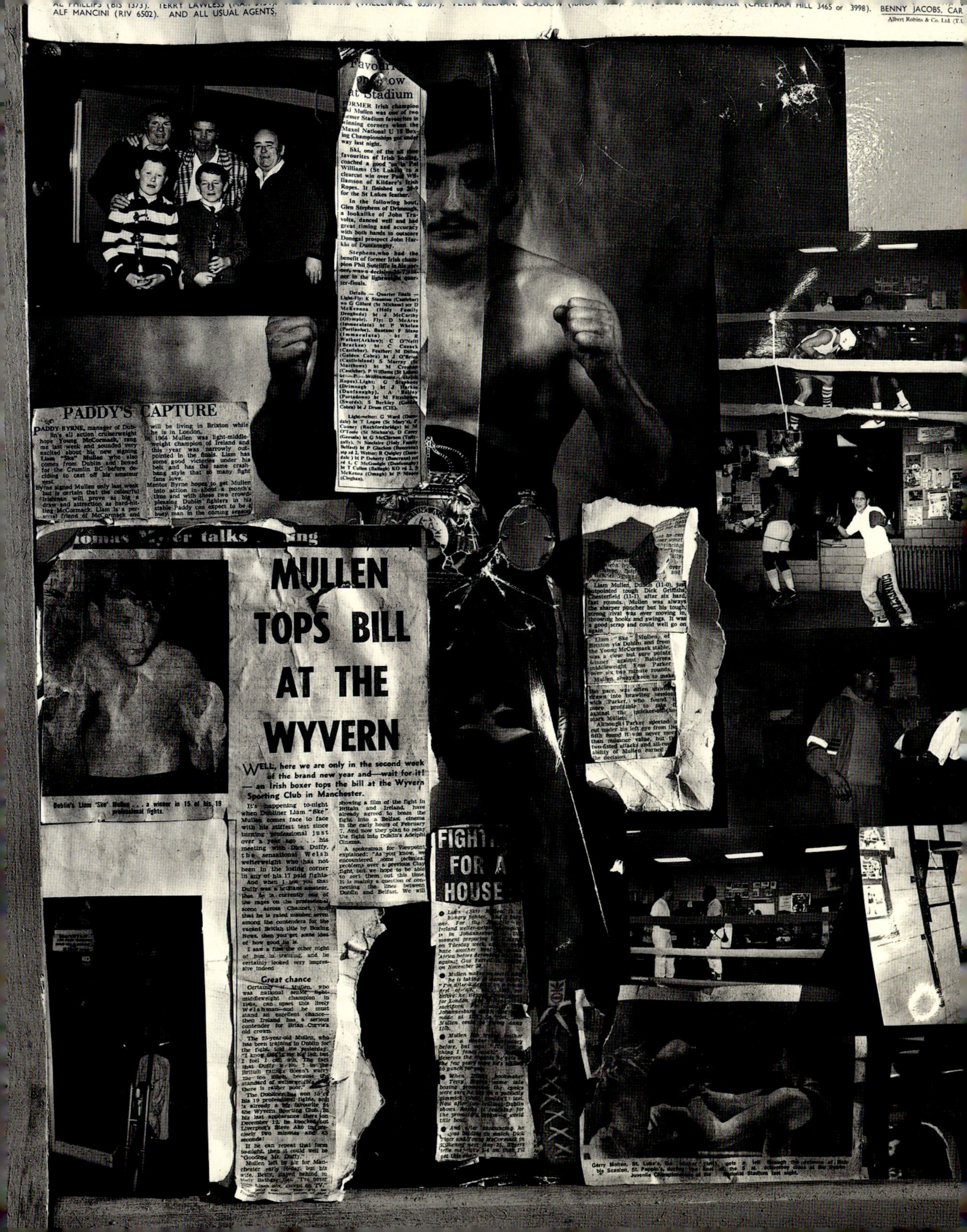
ALF MANCINI (RIV 6502). AND ALL USUAL AGENTS.
BENNY JACOBS, CAR
PADDY'S CAPTURE
PADDY BYRNE, manager of Dublin's all action cruiserweight hope Young McCormack, rang me last week and sounded very excited about his new signing Liam "Ske" Mullen who also comes from Dublin and boxed for the Crumlin BC before deciding to cast off his amateur vest.
Byrne signed Mullen only last week but is certain that the colourful Irishman will prove as big a draw and attraction as hard-hitting McCormack. Liam is a personal friend of McCormack and will be living in Brixton while he is in London.
In 1964 Mullen was light-middleweight champion of Ireland and this year was narrowly outpointed in the finals. Liam has some good victories under his belt and has the same crash-bang style that so many fight fans love.
Mentor Byrne hopes to get Mullen into action in about a month's time and with these two crowd-pleasing Dublin fighters in his stable Paddy can expect to be a busy man in the coming season.
talks
MULLEN TOPS BILL AT THE WYVERN
WELL, here we are only in the second week of the brand new year and—wait for it! — an Irish boxer tops the bill at the Wyvern Sporting Club in Manchester.
It's happening to-night when Dubliner Liam "Ske" Mullen comes face to face with his stiffest test since turning professional just over a year ago . . . his meeting with Dick Duffy, the sensational Welsh welterweight who has not been in the losing corner in any of his 17 paid fights.
I saw a film the other night of him in training, and he certainly looked very impressive indeed
showing a film of the fight in Britain and Ireland, have already agreed to beam the fight into a Belfast cinema in the early hours of February 7. And now they plan to relay the fight into Dublin's Adelphi Cinema.
Great chance
Dublin's Liam 'Ske' Mullen . . . a winner in 15 of his 19 professional fights.
FIGHT
FOR A
HOUSE

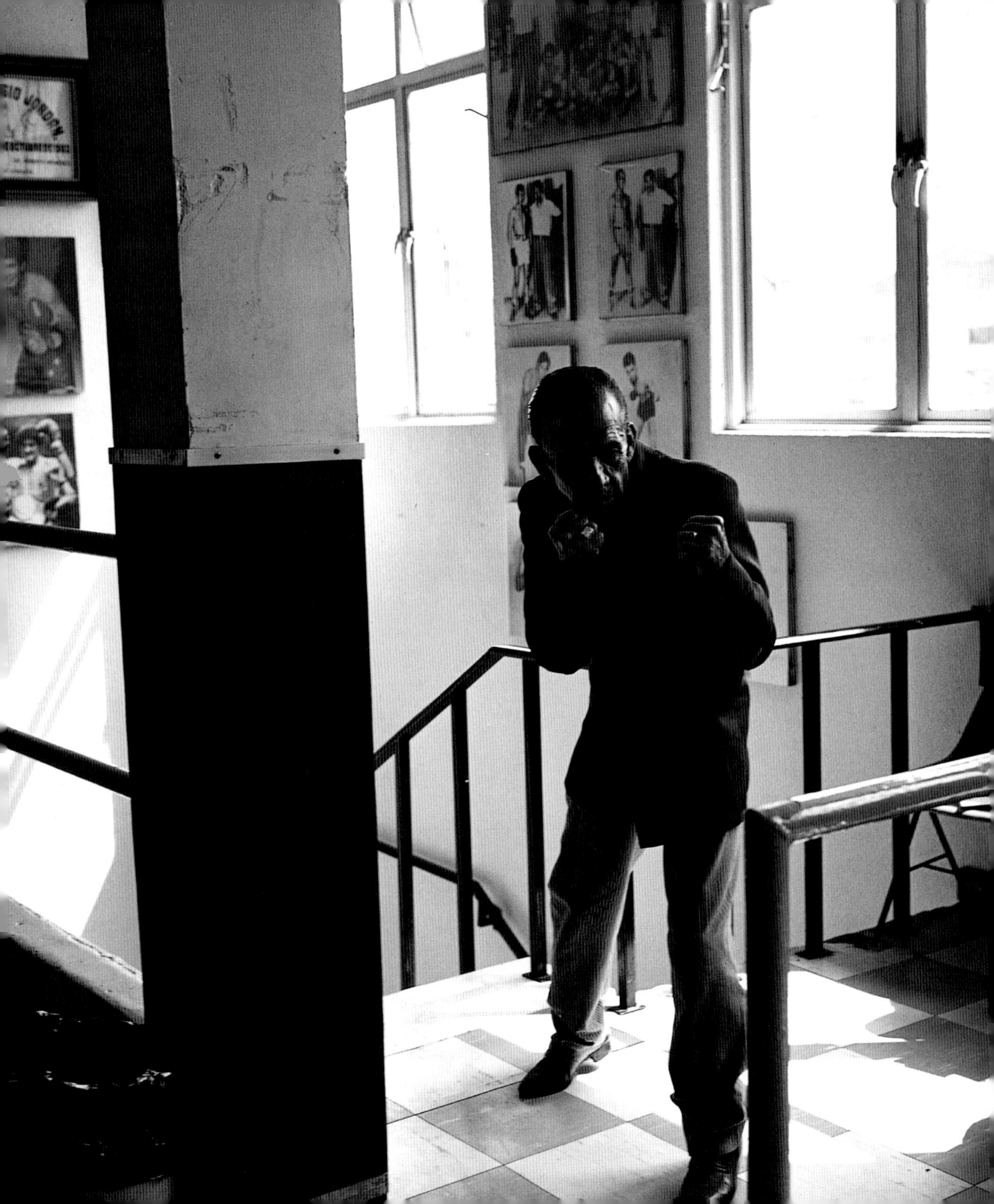

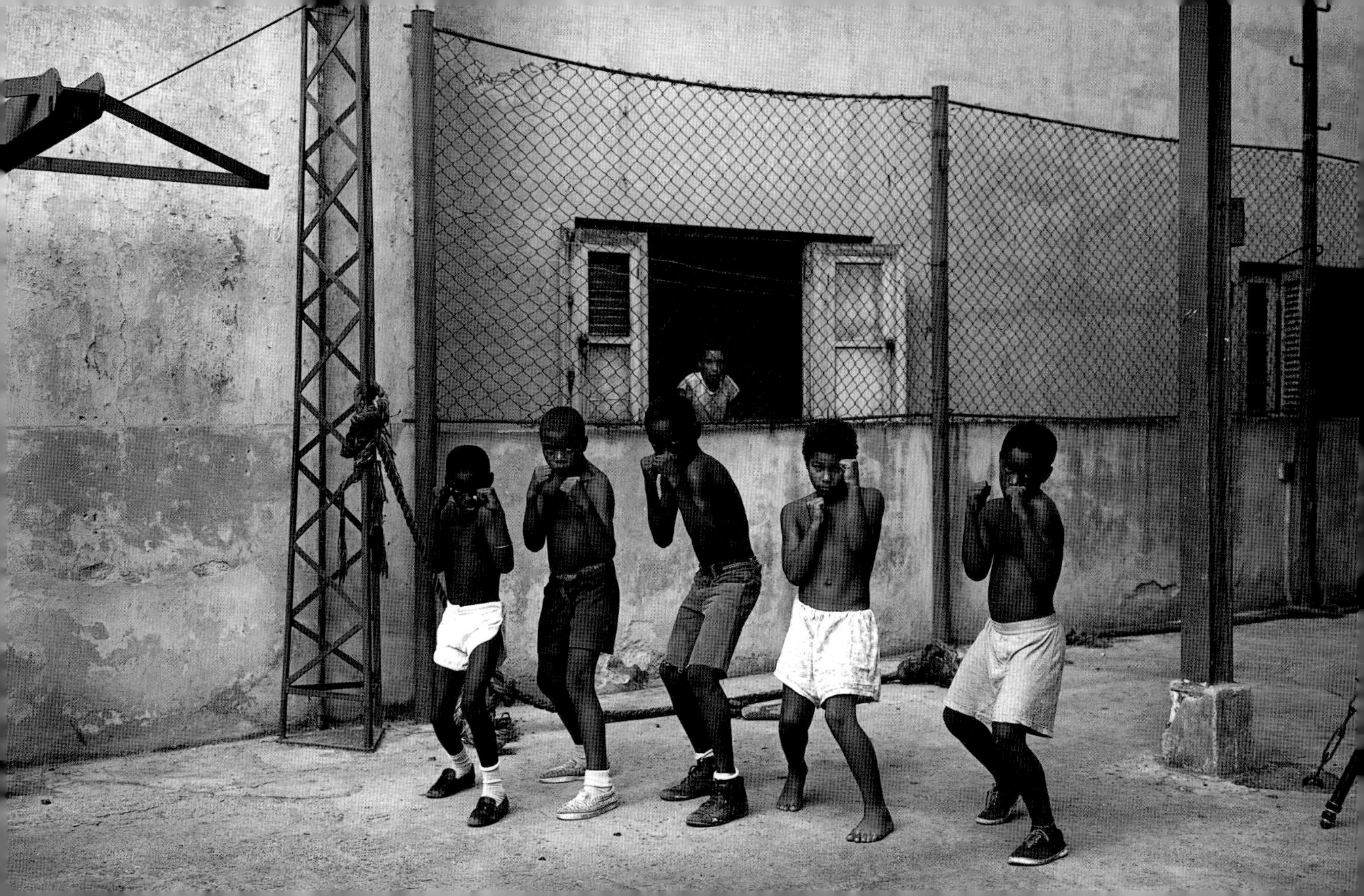

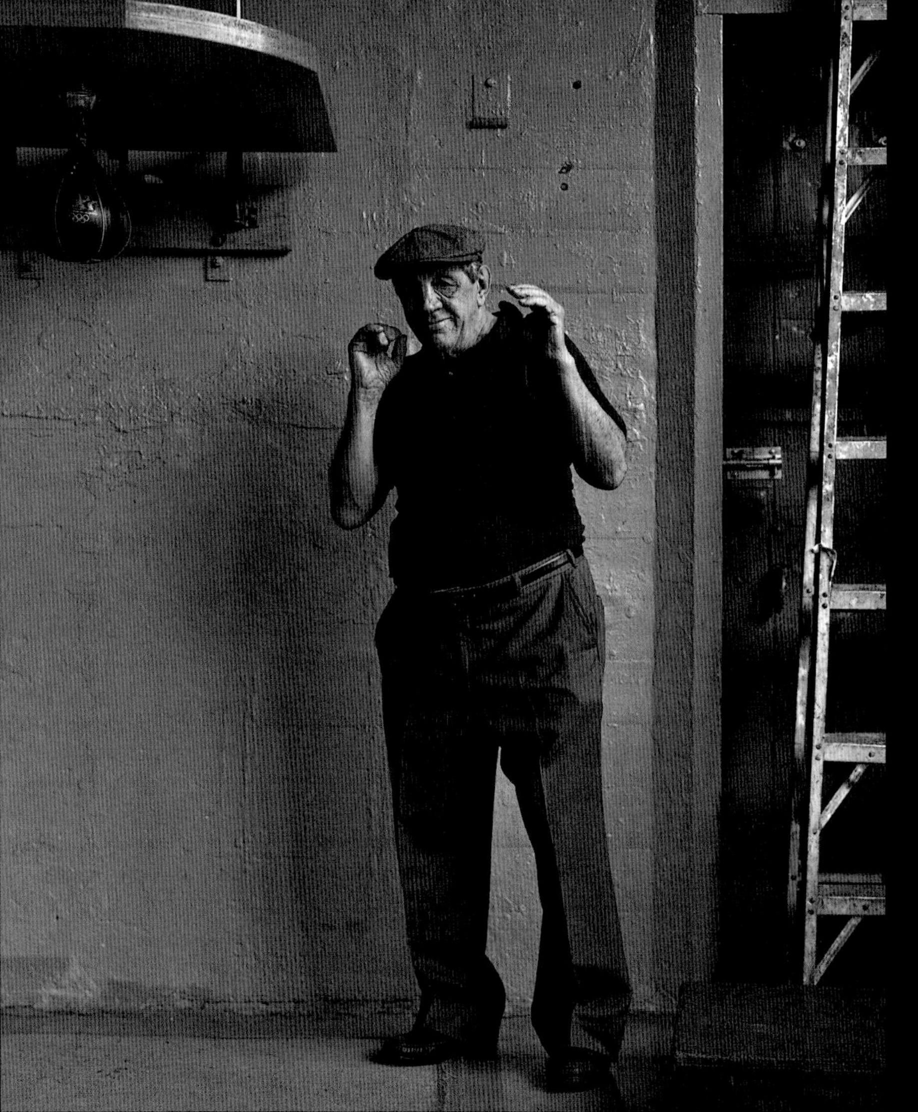

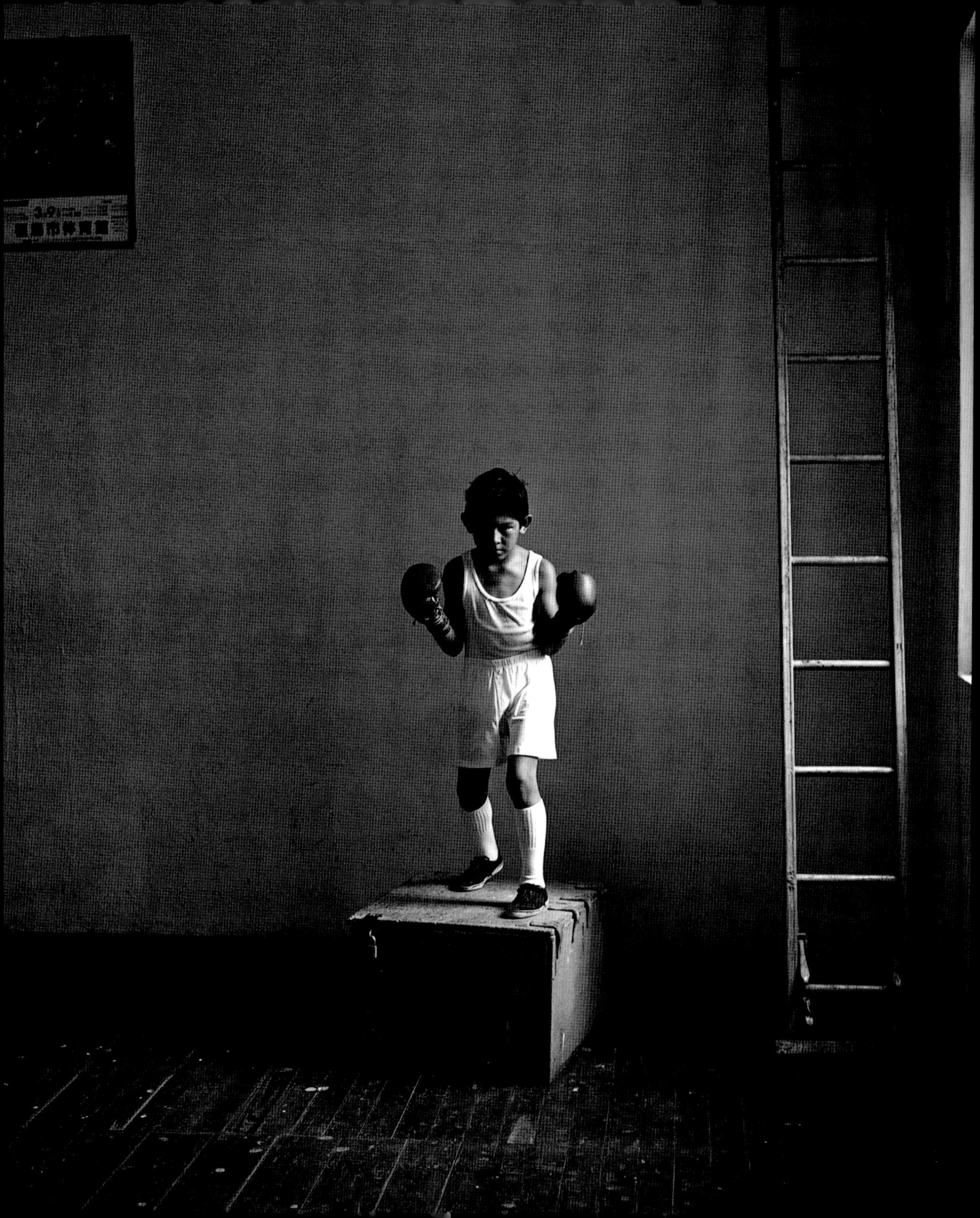
3.9

Once, down on Lexington Avenue and Ninety-sixth Street, my younger brother and I were accosted by a pair of kids a couple of years older, perhaps eleven or twelve. They were nervous about what they were going to do. We were coming back from Sunday School. They demanded our money, backing us against a wall, and my brother shot his fists up––they were about the size of plums—in a classic old-time-fighter's stance, like a miniature Jem Mace in the boxing prints, but I said, No, no, no, and I forked over the twenty cents that was left over from busfare. The shame of it lasts to this day.

GEORGE PLIMPTON

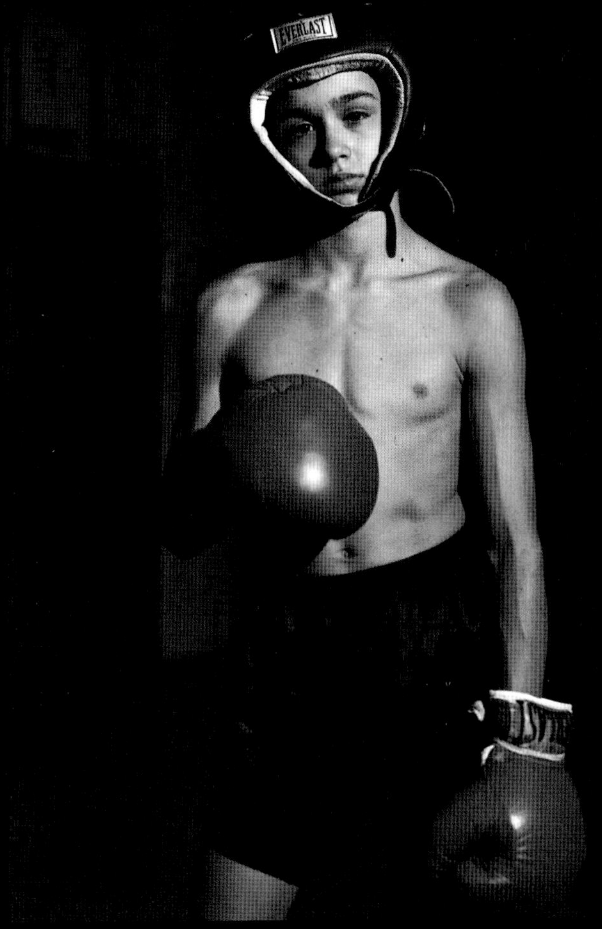
EVERLAST

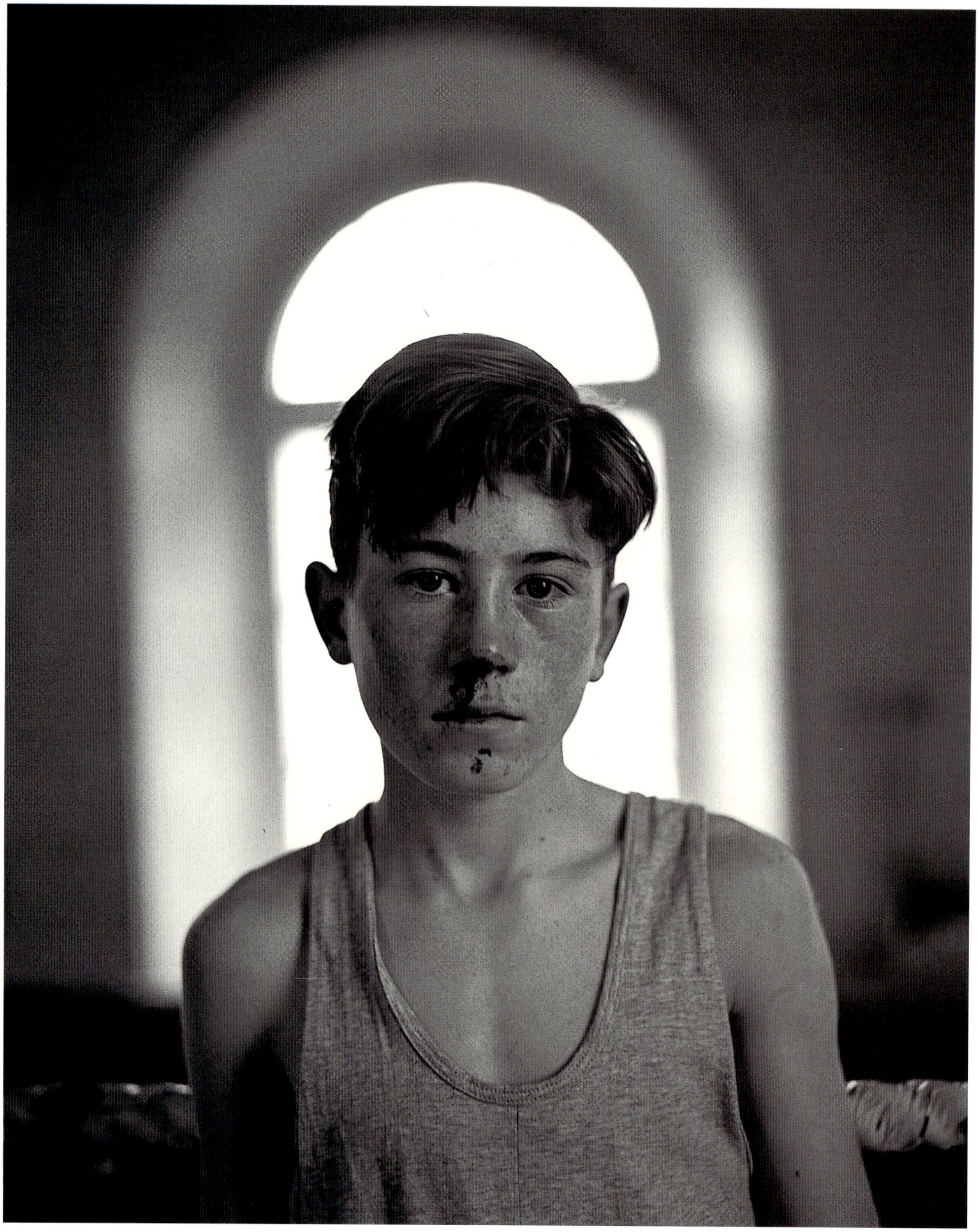

BOXING SHORTS

WALTER KIRN

In gym class that day the boys boxed. Two fat kids were excused for medical reasons and one kid had religious objections. I envied them. My opponent was a farm kid, Glen. His muscles had knots and ridges, like split wood. Glen knocked me down right away. The force was shocking. I lay there. Glen didn't budge. I left my body.

Then I was on the ceiling, looking down. I saw my body flat on the mat. I couldn't accept I was beaten. I started gasping, pretending to have an asthma attack. The teacher declared Glen the winner and held his arm up. I gasped and gasped, afraid to stop my act. The school nurse came in. "Be a man. Stand up," she said. But I was thirteen. That's not a man. It's nothing.

■

I waited outside the school's back door at lunch time. He was bigger, older. I ambushed him. They watched. I jumped on his back and grabbed his neck and hung there, dragging him to his knees. The girls drew back, the boys moved closer. He still didn't know who'd attacked him. He was yelling. I pounded the sides of his head, his temples. A blow to the windpipe could kill a man. Boys cheered. He didn't fight back as I smashed his nose and throat. After two women teachers broke us up, he licked blood off the mustache he was starting to grow.

■

Our father made me and my brother spar as boys—out in the street, with the neighbors looking down. We didn't use gloves. Our father refused to buy them. Time after time, my brother pounded me. The neighbors booed. They wanted me: the little guy. Pretty soon, my brother got sick of hurting me, but my father wouldn't let us quit. He said that someday one of us would thank him, hinting that it would be me. One day I won one. The neighbors cheered and my father squeezed my shoulder. He asked me if revenge felt good, if victory was worth the wait. I could tell he expected his thanks now. I hit him hard.

■

We hated their town and they hated ours. They drove a pickup truck across our ball field. We drove one across theirs. They spray-painted curse words on our water tower. We slashed some of their tires. It was war. We agreed to meet them in a parking lot, and we drove around for a while first and smoked. Our biggest guy punched his open hand and growled. Our

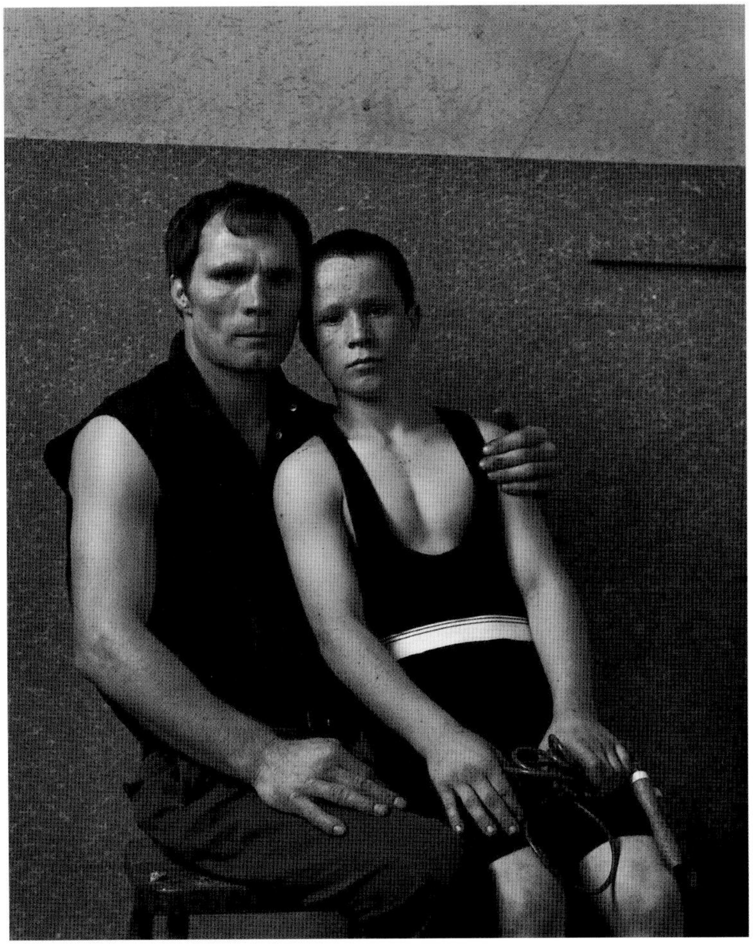

next biggest guy drank vodka. We waited. When the other guys didn't show up, we danced around like we'd won. We hugged each other, and bragged about how afraid of us they were. In the morning we learned that their car had gone off a bridge. Two killed, three injured. It was still a victory.

■

We thought that because he boxed he must be dangerous. We tried never to crowd him at the bar. If he had a strong opinion, we'd agree with him. If he played a song on the jukebox, we'd all dance. We feared he'd snap some night. We almost wanted him to. We wanted to see how quick he really was.

■

On the sidewalk outside the bar on Sunday mornings there was always blood and vomit. I couldn't wait until I was old enough for some of it to be mine.

■

I hit the gym long before sunrise. It's peaceful then. The floors are slippery, freshly mopped. The shower heads drip and echo. I jump some rope. I sing along with the radio, maybe, or make up tricky dance steps. Outside, it's dark and I picture the other

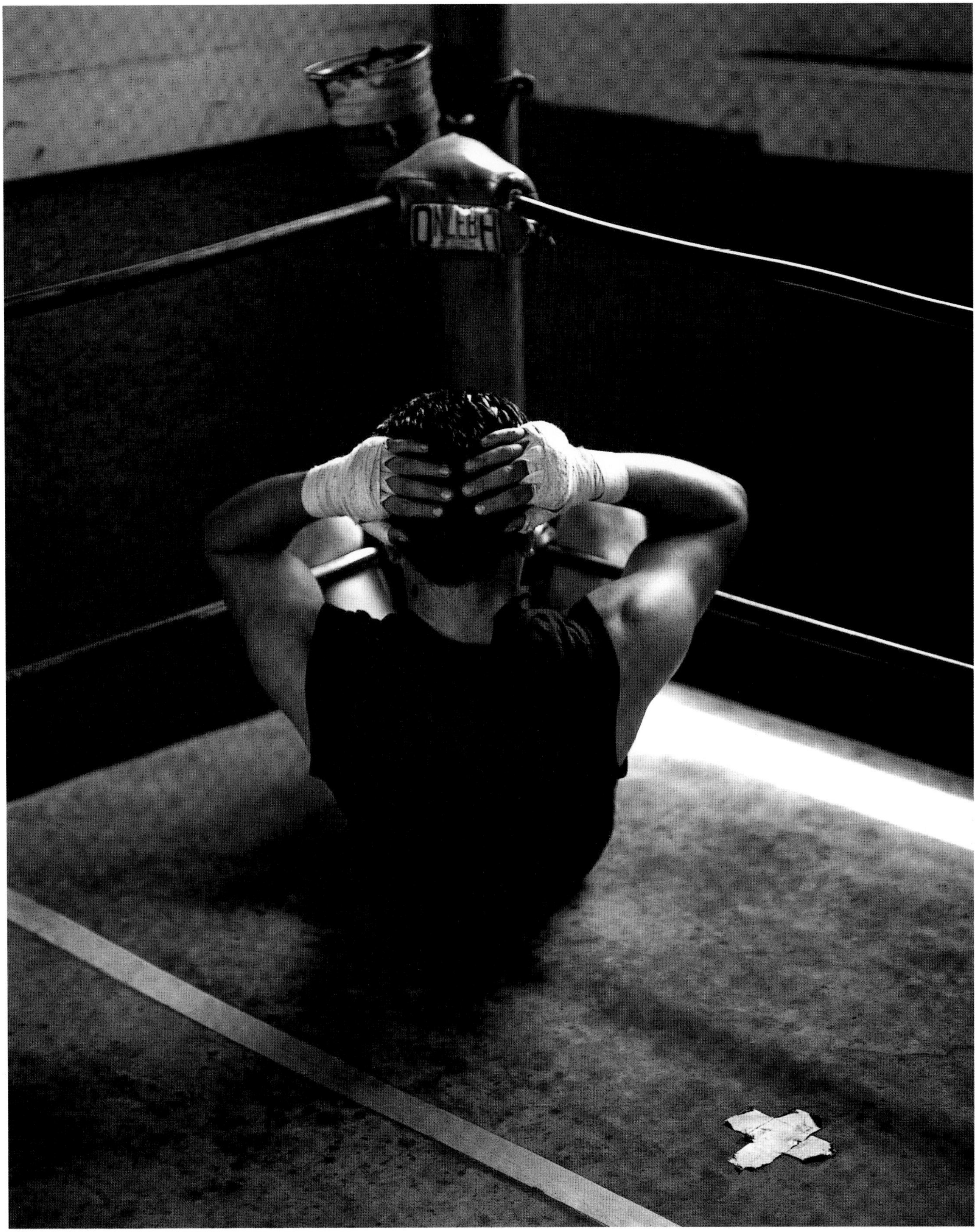

fighters just waking up, slipping out of women's beds. They pee, and rub on shaving cream, knowing I'm already out here, working, sweating. When they finally show up, they duck past me into the locker room. The same way I did when I was a loser.

■

Rituals. Superstitions. A crucifix at the bottom of your locker. No friends or family in the first three rows. Breathe out when you're weighed, breathe in when you're announced. Touch a boy baby. Avoid old women's eyes. Stare at the mirror, imagining you're the other man. Kiss his face where you want your fists to hurt it.

■

Once I woke up and couldn't feel my tongue. Once all the joints in my body filled up with fluid. Once I forgot the names for all the colors. Once I could have sworn I heard my brain come loose and smash the sides of my skull. Once I almost quit.

■

I loved the robe, the shiny trunks, the shoes. I felt pretty in them, like a lady. I admit it. When I held out my hands and men laced up my gloves, I knew what it was like to be adored.

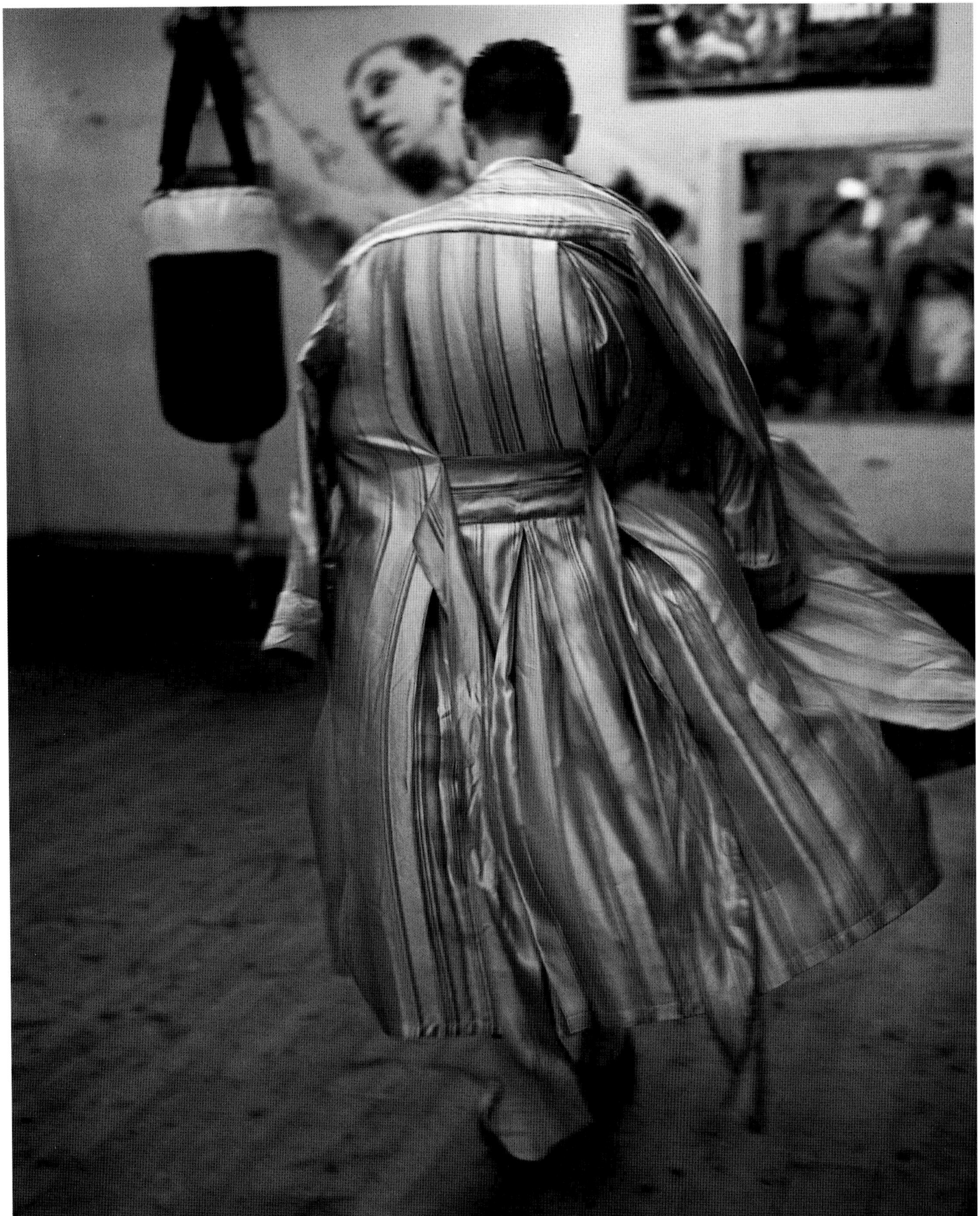

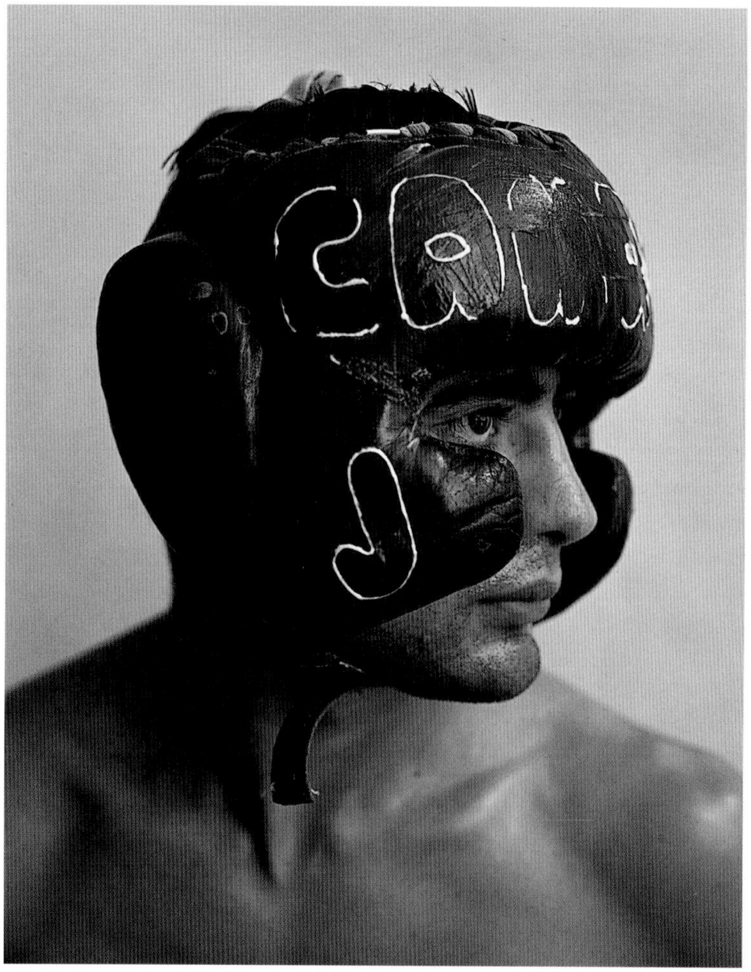

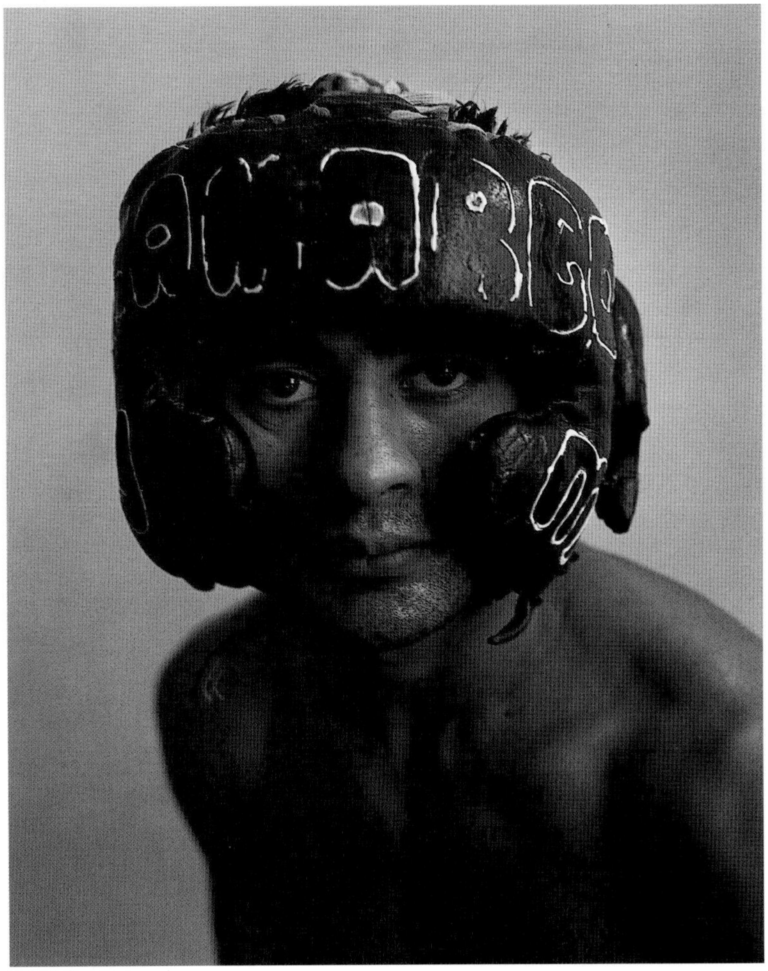

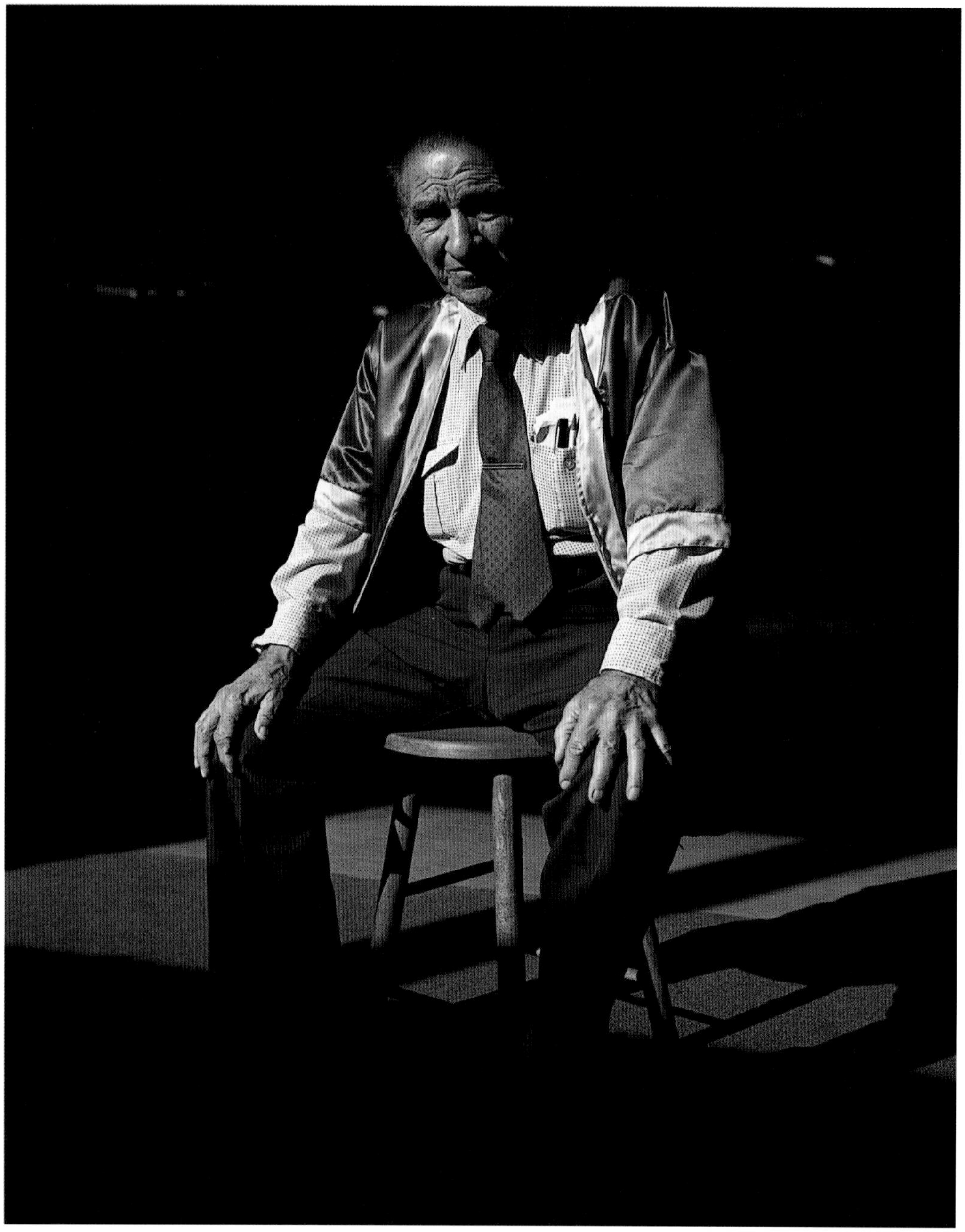

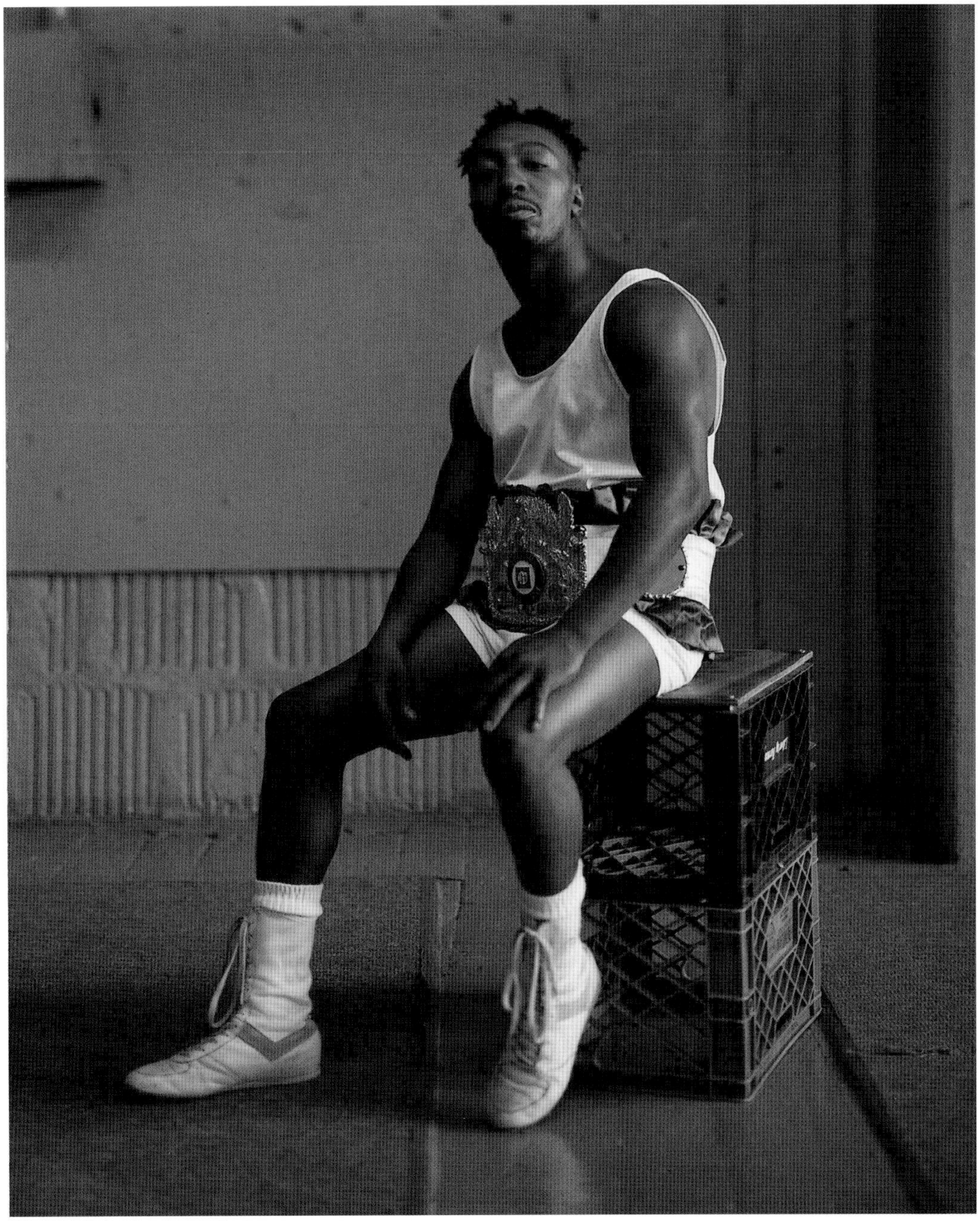

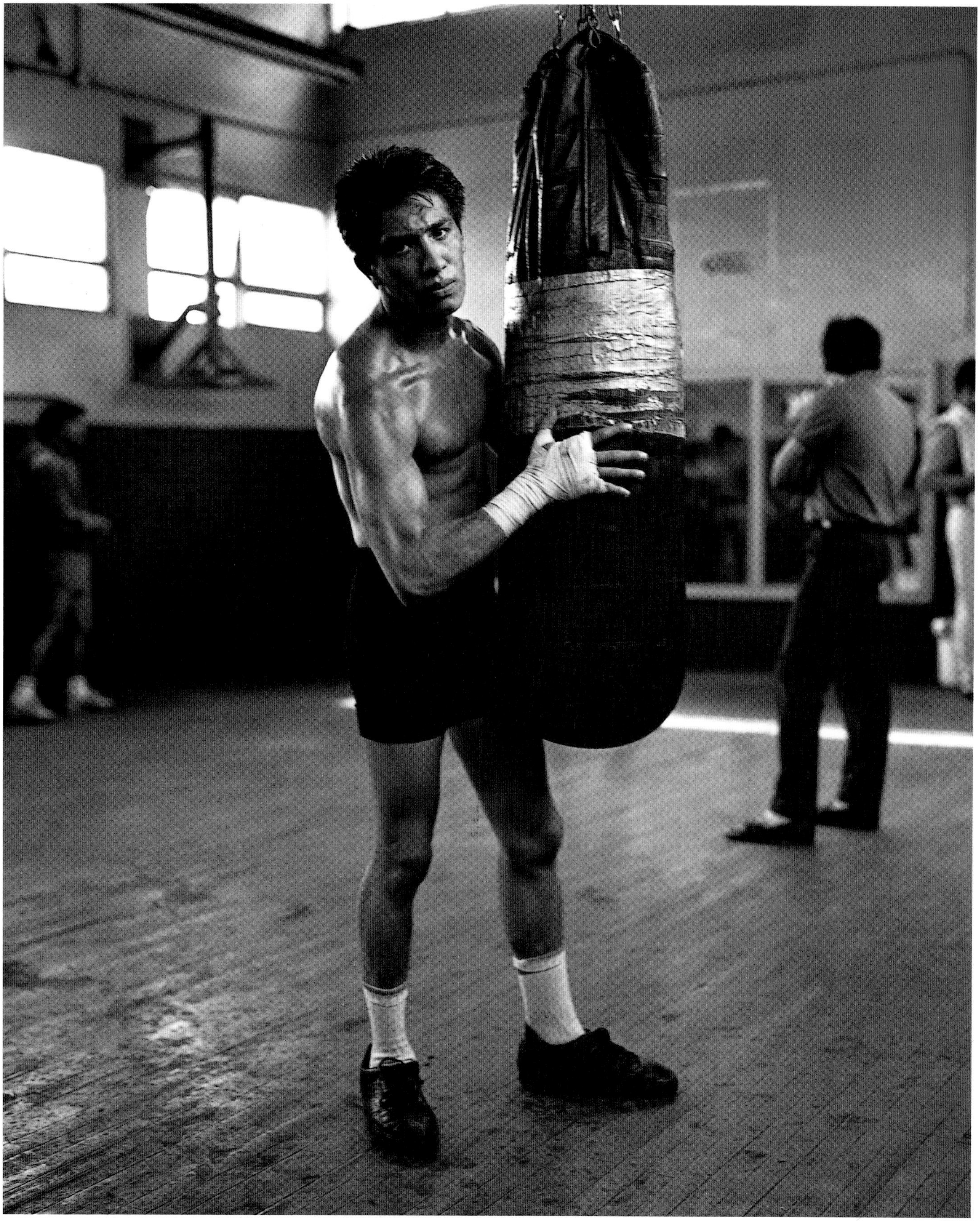

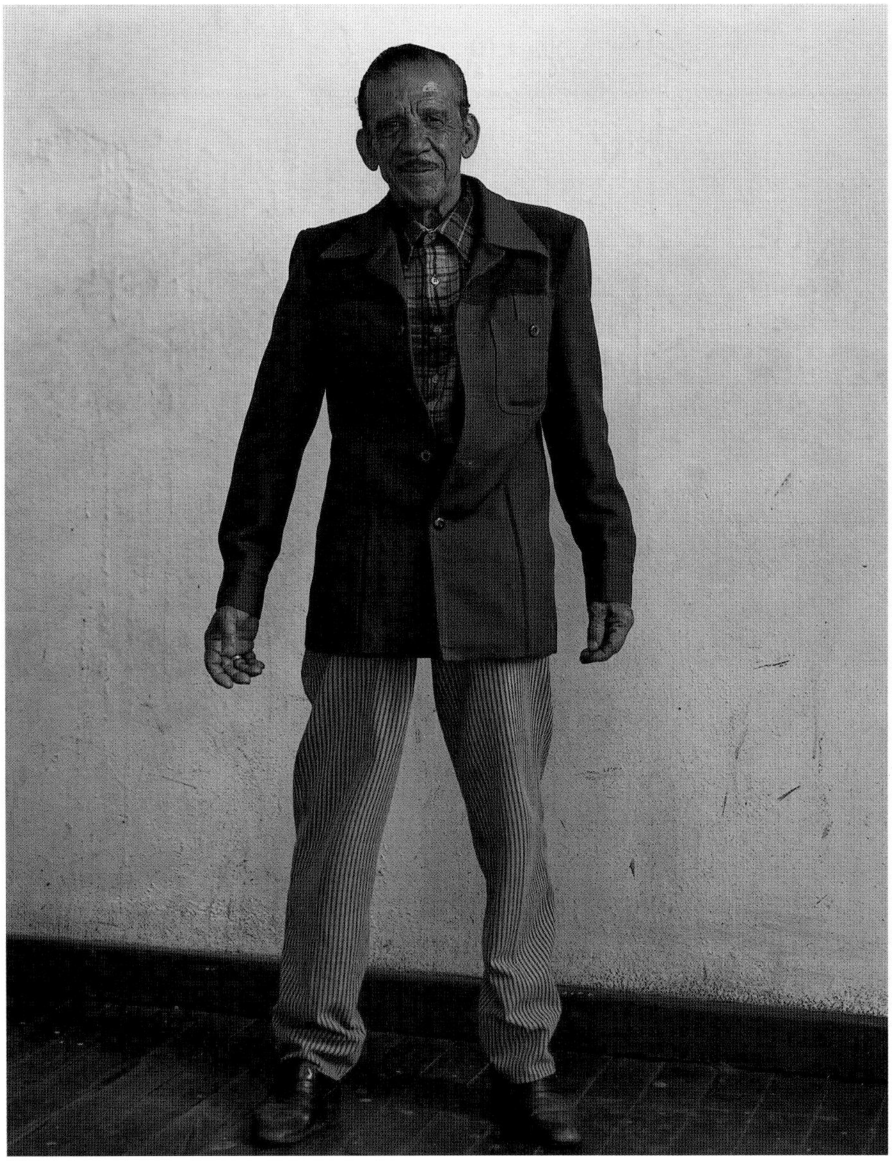

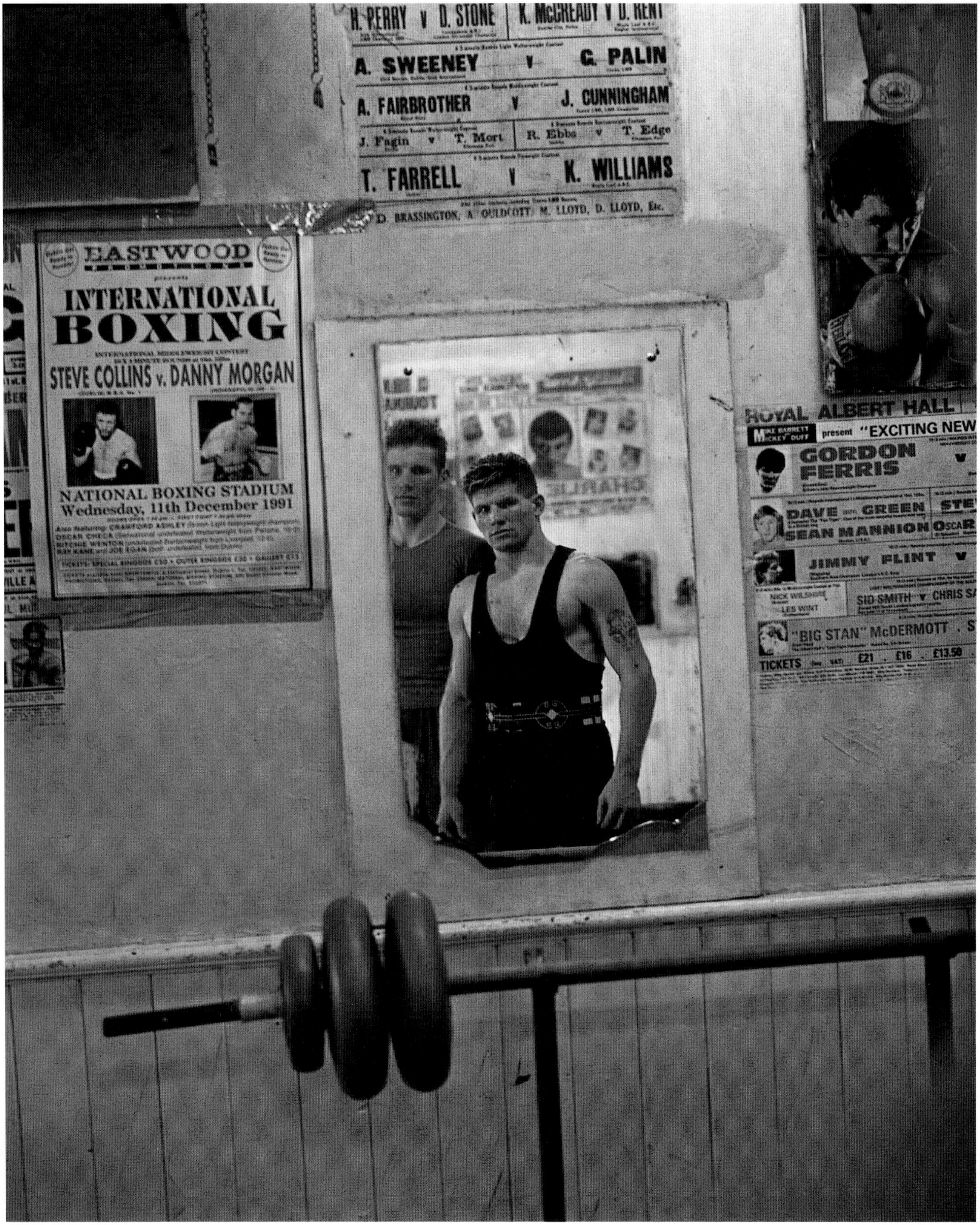
H. PERRY v D. STONE
K. McCREADY v D. KENT
A. SWEENEY v G. PALIN
A. FAIRBROTHER v J. CUNNINGHAM
J. Fagin v T. Mort
R. Ebbs v T. Edge
T. FARRELL v K. WILLIAMS
D. BRASSINGTON, A. OULDCOTT, M. LLOYD, D. LLOYD, Etc.
EASTWOOD
presents
INTERNATIONAL BOXING
STEVE COLLINS v. DANNY MORGAN
NATIONAL BOXING STADIUM
Wednesday, 11th December 1991
ROYAL ALBERT HALL
present "EXCITING NEW
GORDON FERRIS
DAVE GREEN
SEAN MANNION
JIMMY FLINT
SID SMITH v CHRIS SA
"BIG STAN" McDERMOTT
TICKETS
£21 . £16 . £13.50

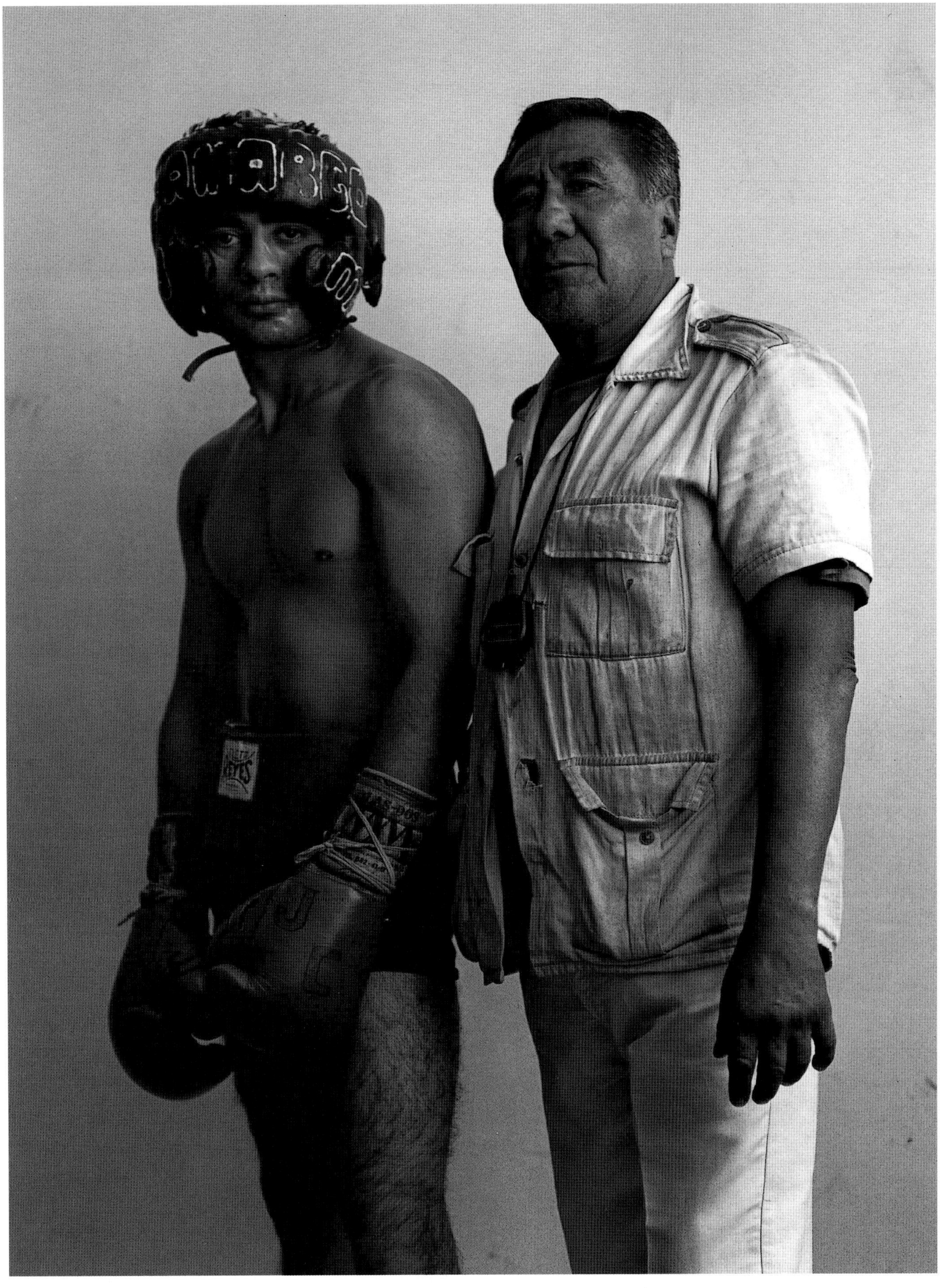

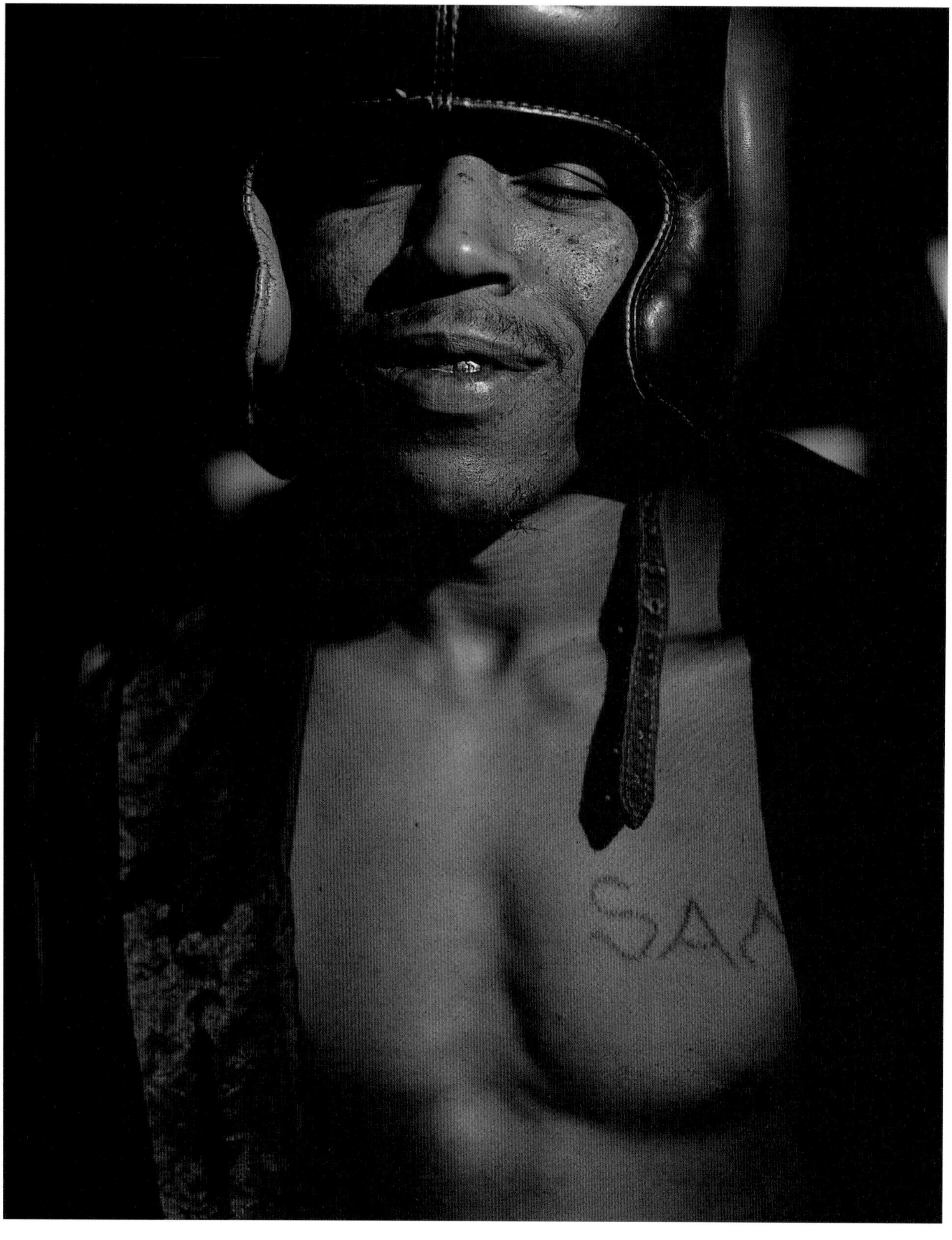

Hoping never done nothing. It *wanting* that do it. You got to want to win so bad you can taste it. If you want to win bad enough you win. They no way in hell this dude going beat me. He too old. I going be all over him. I going kick his ass so bad, every time he take a bite of food tomorrow he going think of me. He be one sore son-of-a-bitch. He going *know* he been in a fight. I get him before he get me. I going hit him with everything. I won't just *beat* that motherfucker, I going *kill* him.

LEONARD GARDNER

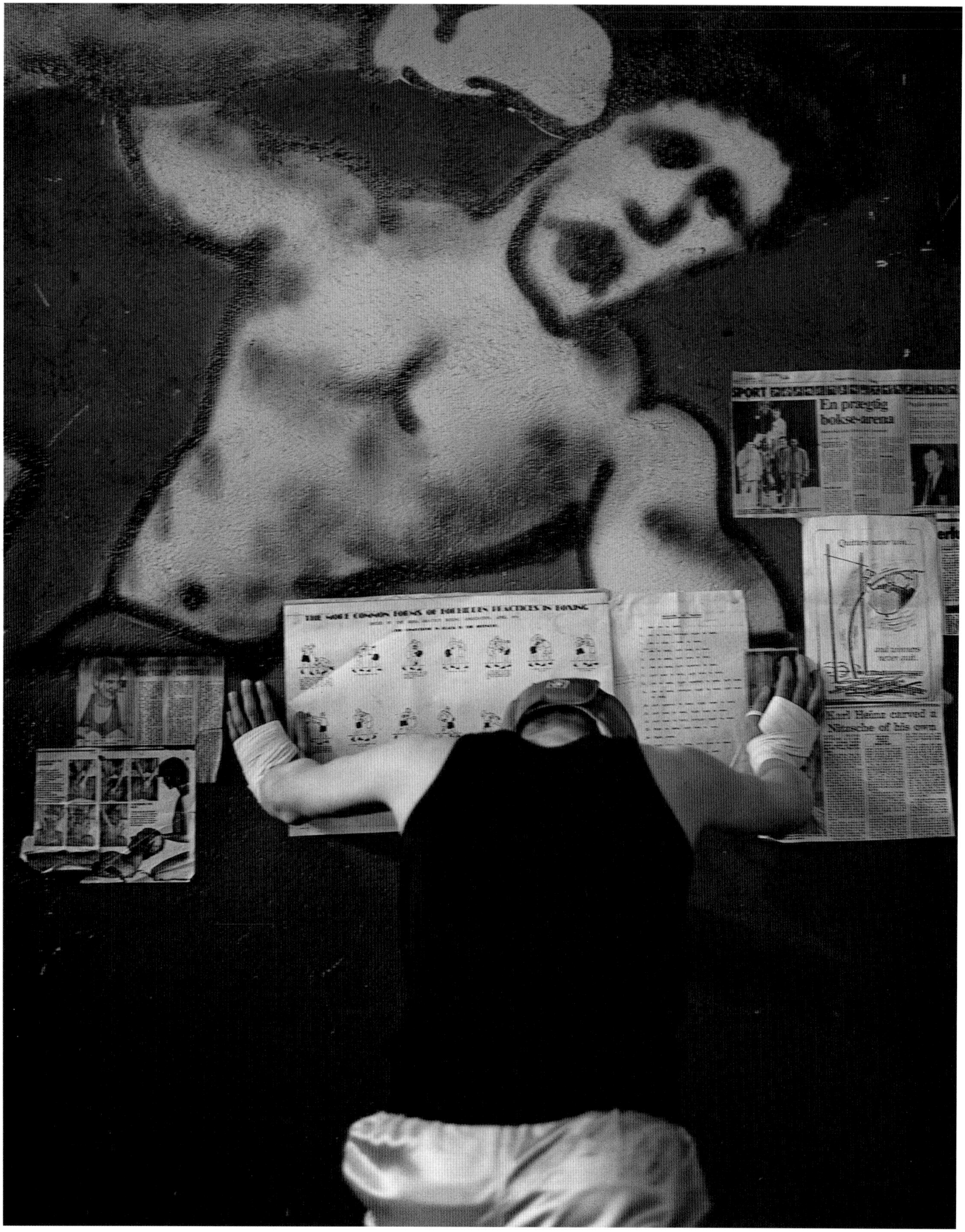

SPORT
En prægtig bokse-arena
THE MOST COMMON FORMS OF FORBIDDEN PRACTICES IN BOXING
Karl Heinz carved a Nitzsche of his own

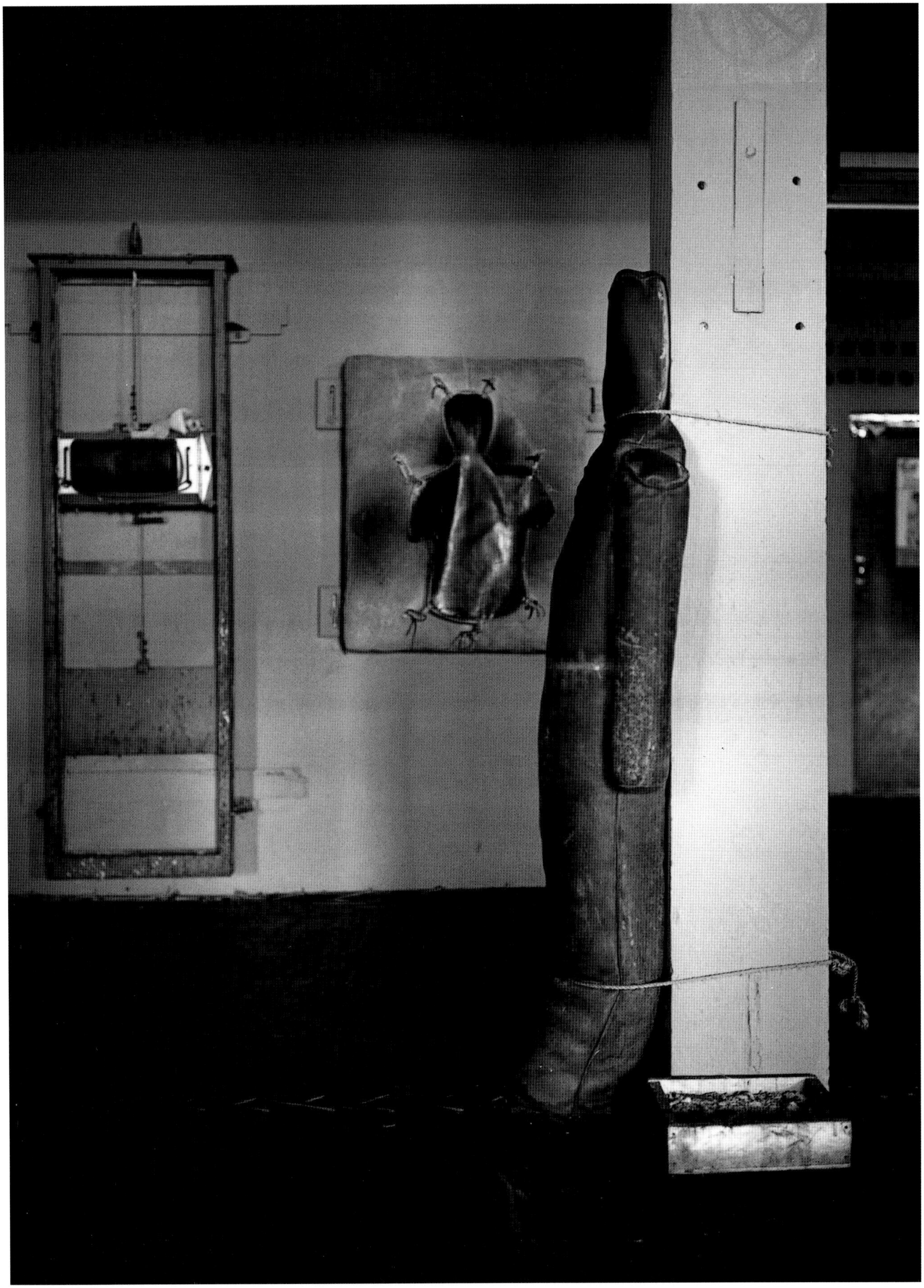

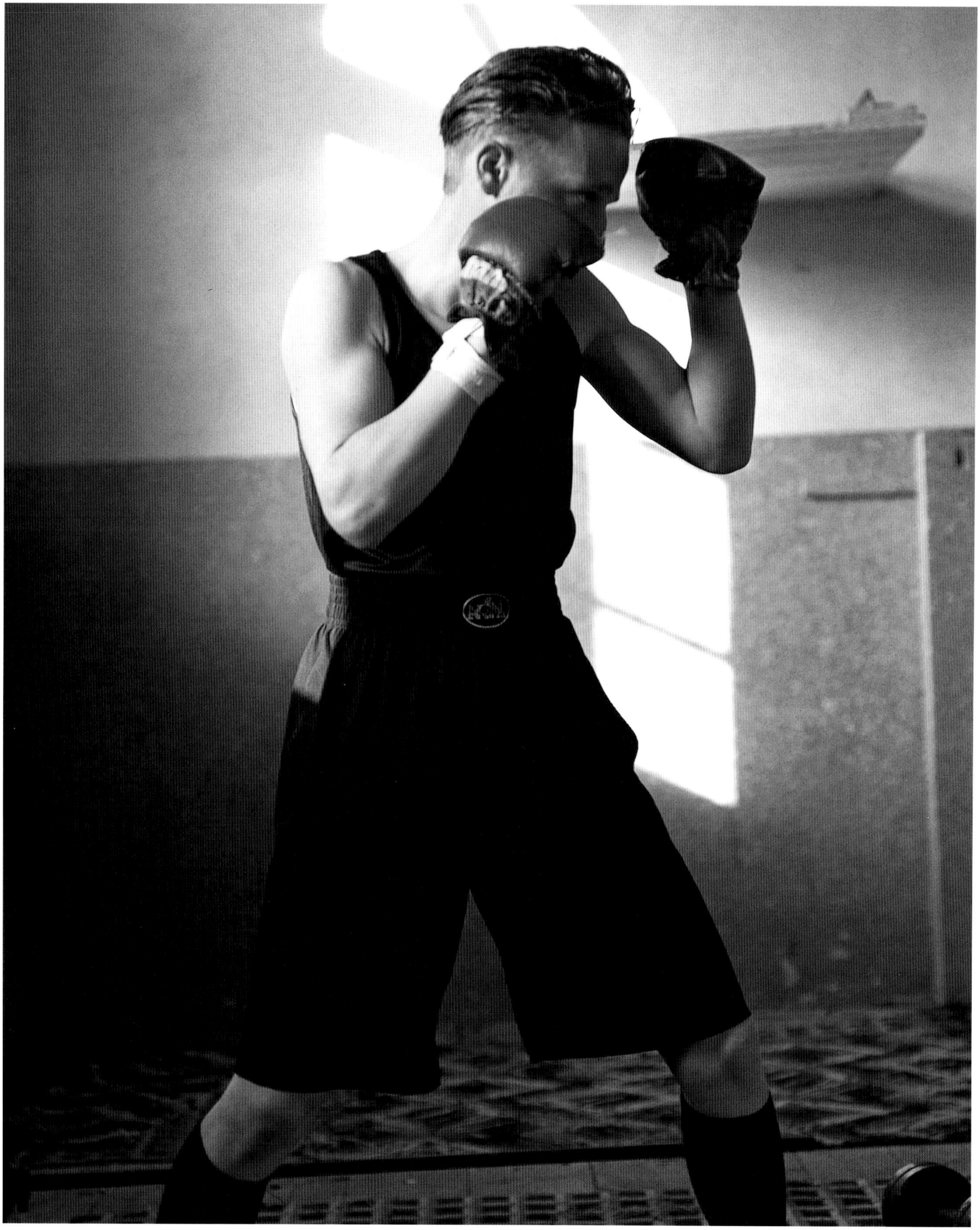

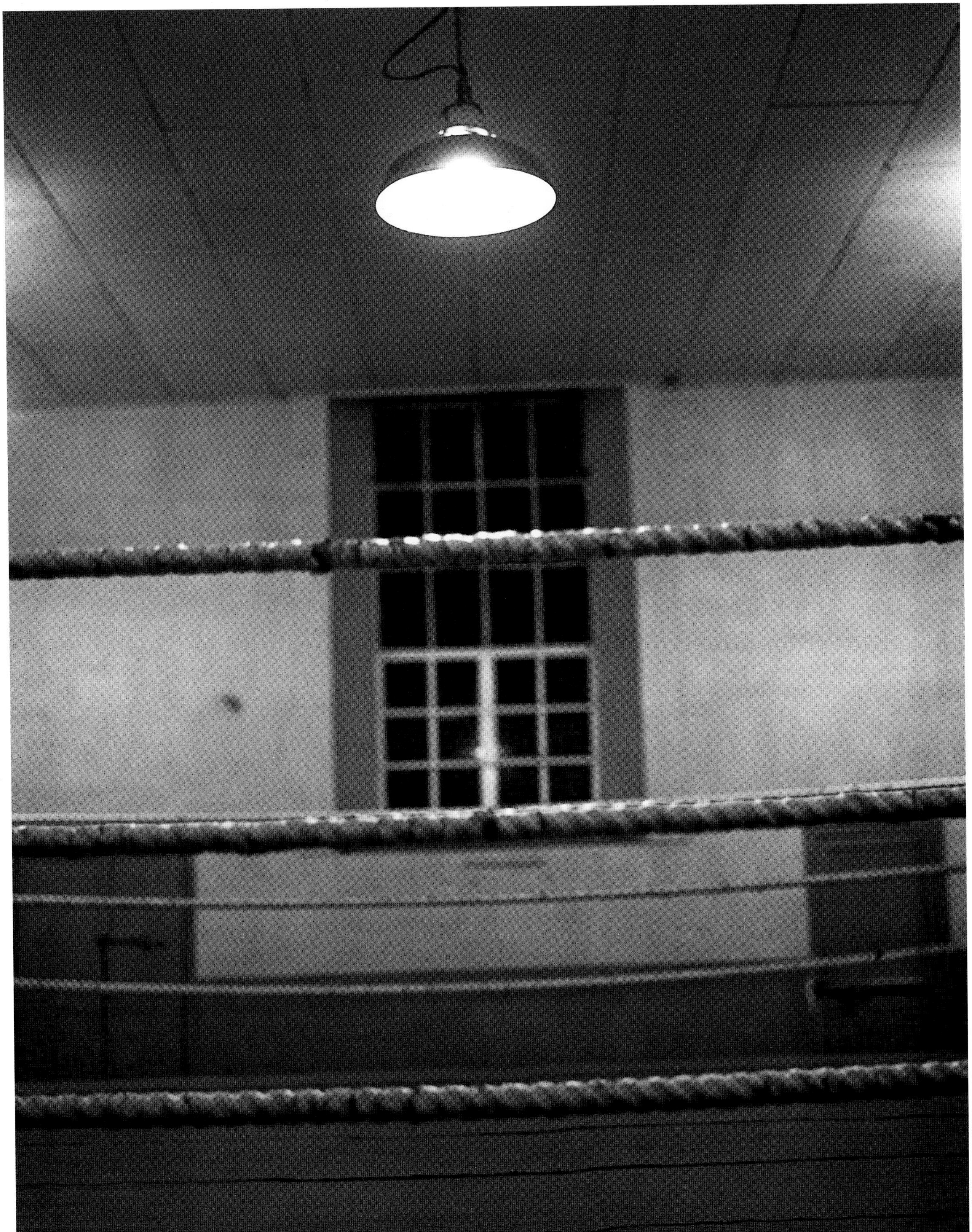

Slouched unhappily in his corner for the windup, he watched the lights overhead swaying a little, and closed his eyes. When he opened them, a slow dust was rising toward the lights. He saw it sweep suddenly, swift and sidewise, high over the ropes and out across the dark and watchful rows. Below him someone pushed the warning buzzer.

NELSON ALGREN

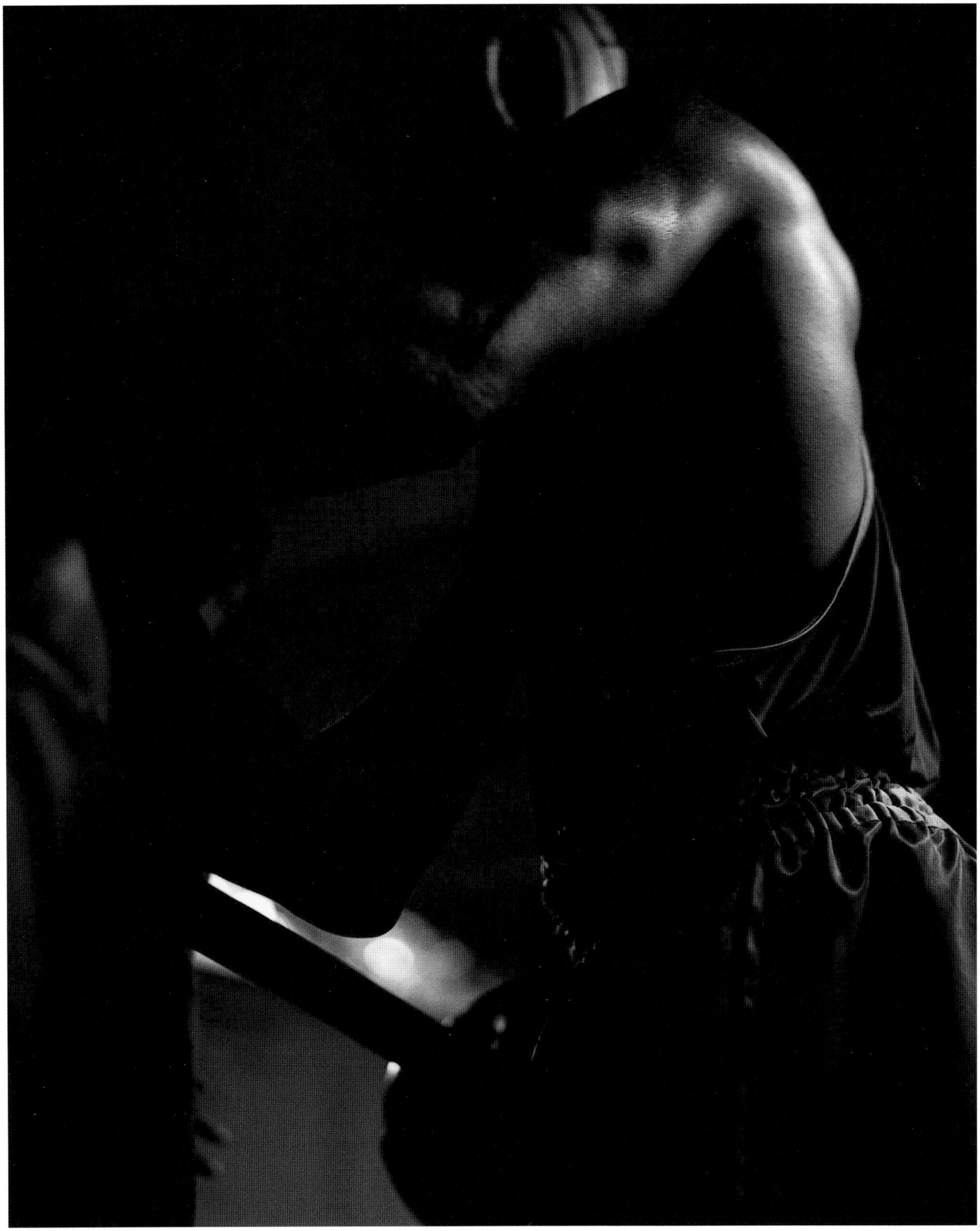

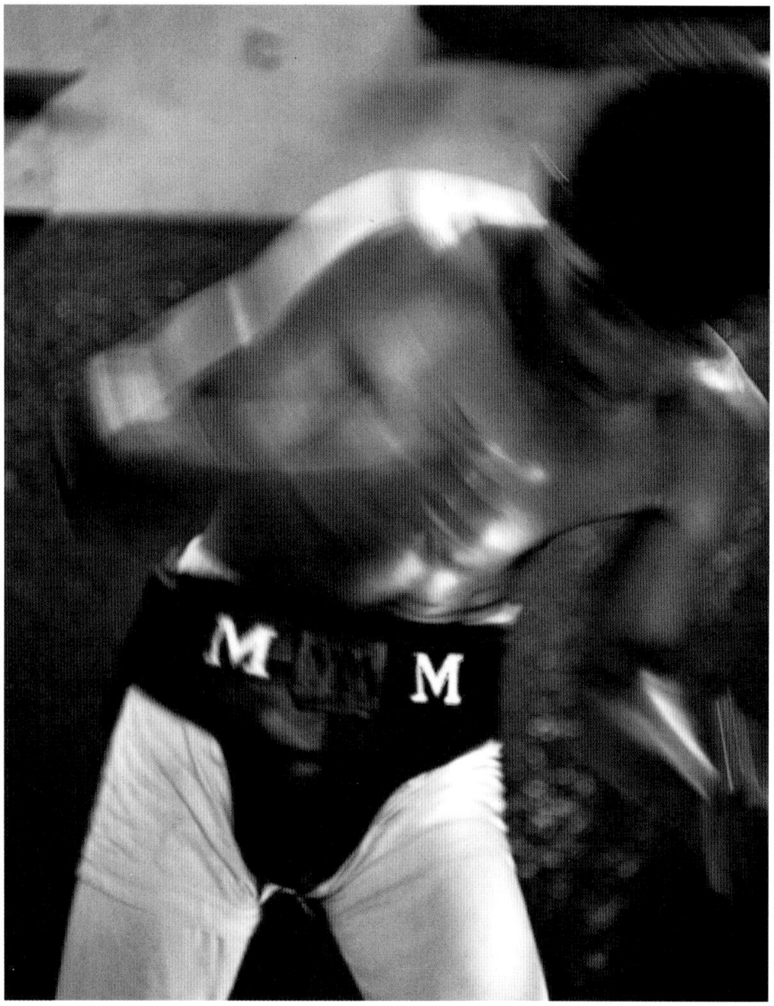
M
M

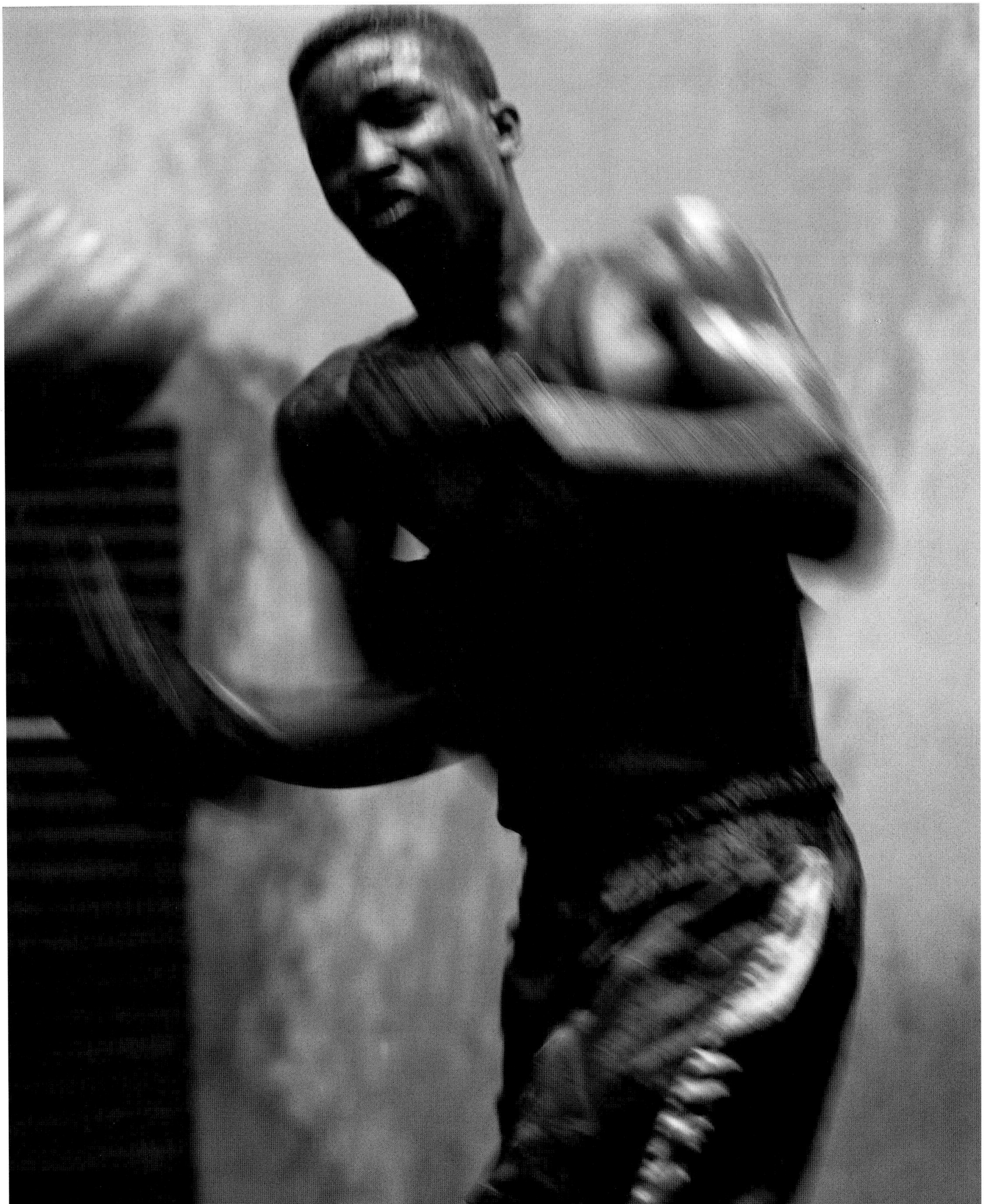

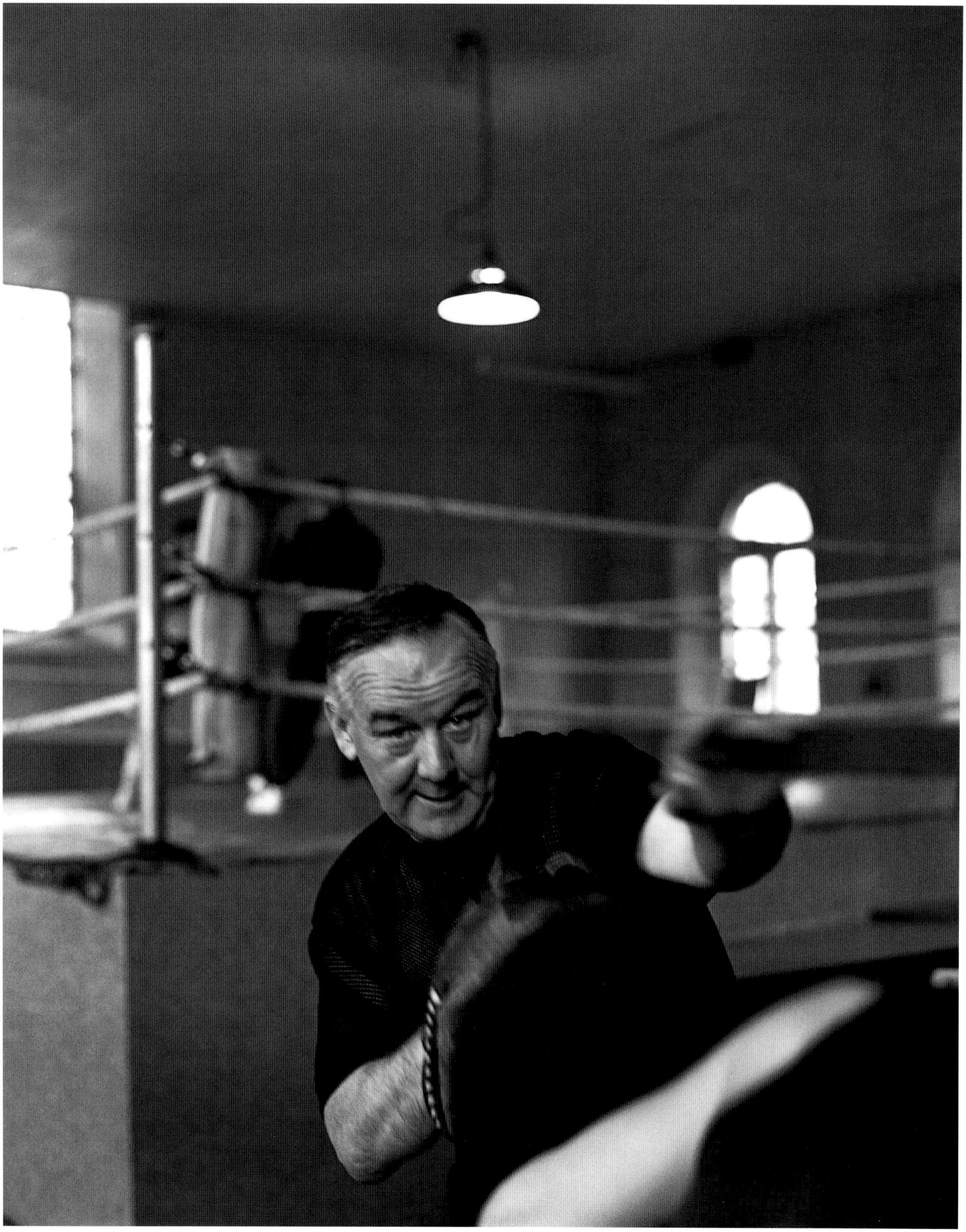

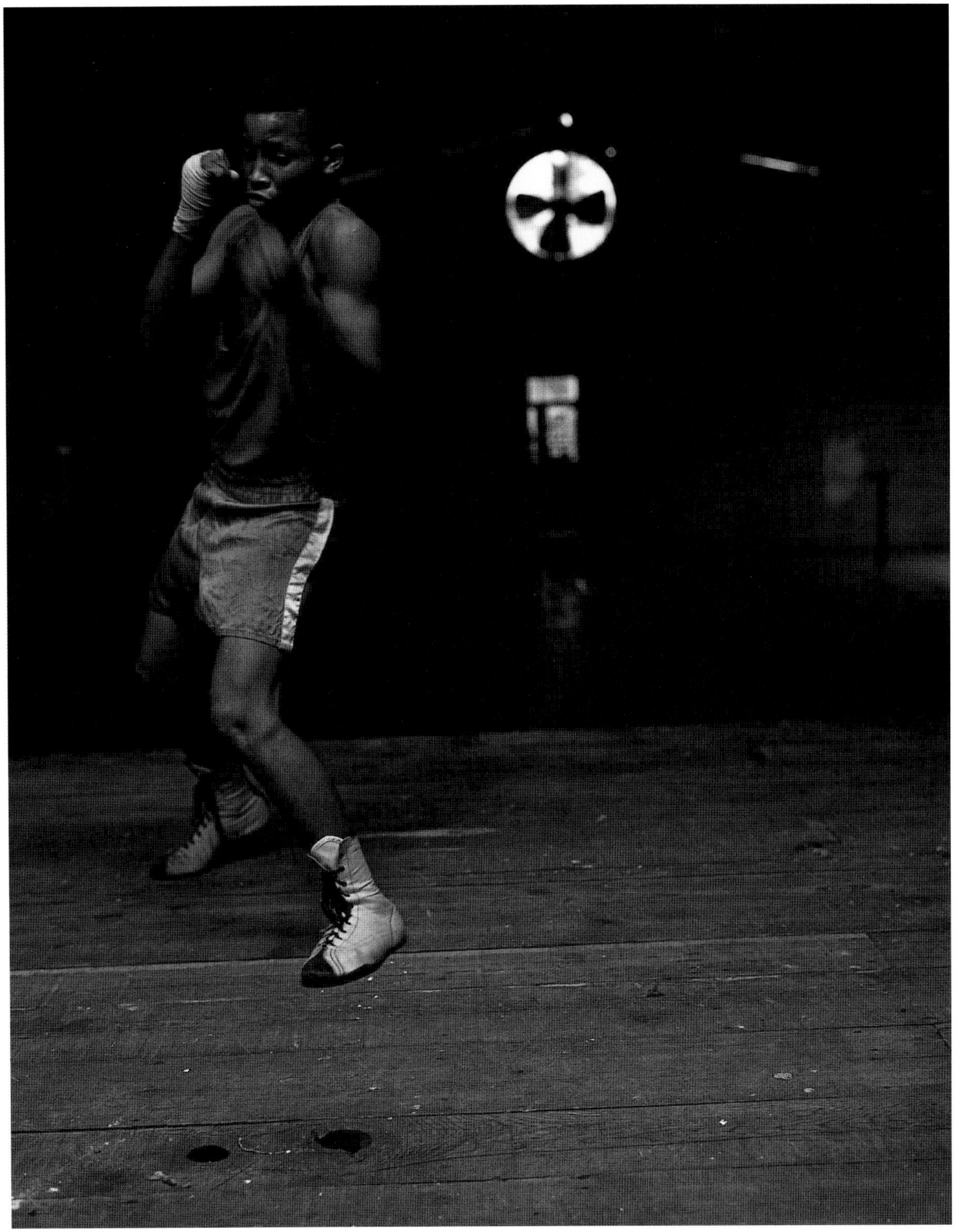

I finished the guy off with a shot to the temple. He sat there against the post, in a daze. All the characters in the overcoats were crowding in down by the ring. All the phones were ringing and nobody paid no attention. I hopped out through the ropes. Some trainer jumped into the ring to tend to the guy with the Spanish name. The joint was kind of jumping there for a minute. Terry was whacking me on the back.

ROCKY GRAZIANO & ROWLAND BARBER

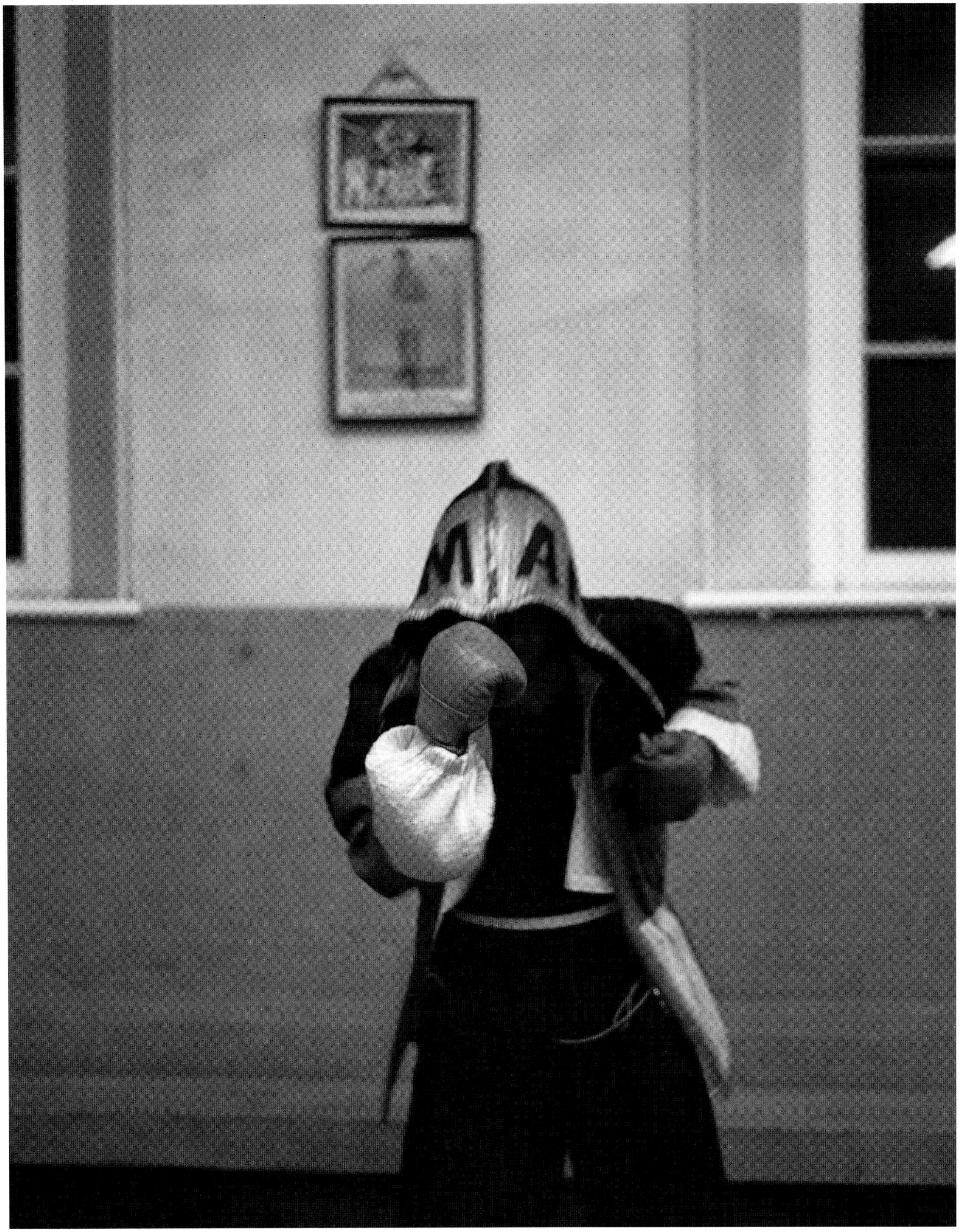

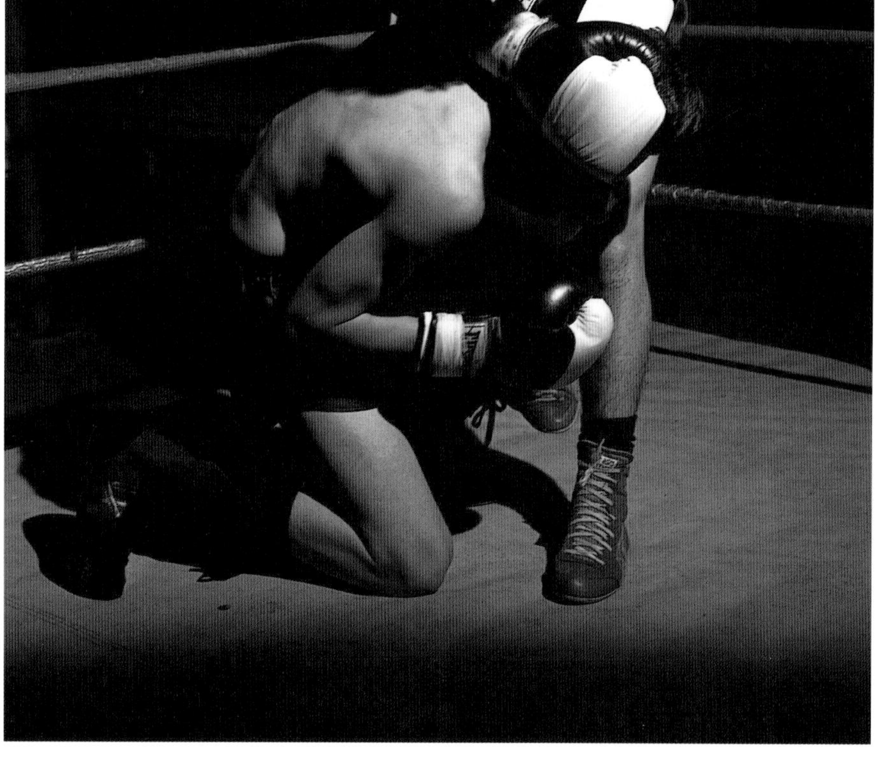

That period had been the peak of his life, though he had not realized it then. It had gone by without time for reflection, ending while he was still thinking things were going to get better. He had not realized the ability and local fame he had then was all he was going to have. Nor had his manger realized it when he moved him up to opponents of national importance. That knowledge had been mercilessly pounded into Tully in a half dozen bouts as he swung and missed and staggered, eyes closed to slits. Then he had looked to his wife for some indefinable endorsement, some solicitous comprehension of the pain and sacrifice he felt he endured for her sake, some always withheld recognition of the rites of virility. Waiting, he drank. After six months he fought once more and was knocked out by a man of no importance at all. Then he began to wish for someone who could give him back that newly-wed wholeness and ease, but it was a feeling he could not find again, and he knew now that his mistake had been in thinking he could. That was how he had lost her—by looking for it. Without her he could not get up in the morning.

LEONARD GARDNER

She had never, at any time, thought it would be like this. When she was still so young she had listened to the words of Frank Sinatra, but she had always known those were not the truth and that it would never be like that. She had not thought about it much, just that when she did get married it would probably be to some ordinary working guy, and they would live in a little apartment. She could never have known that it would be with a fighter and that they would have two cars and live in their own house, and that she would be driven from it periodically, from her own house, by voices like this.

W.C. HEINZ

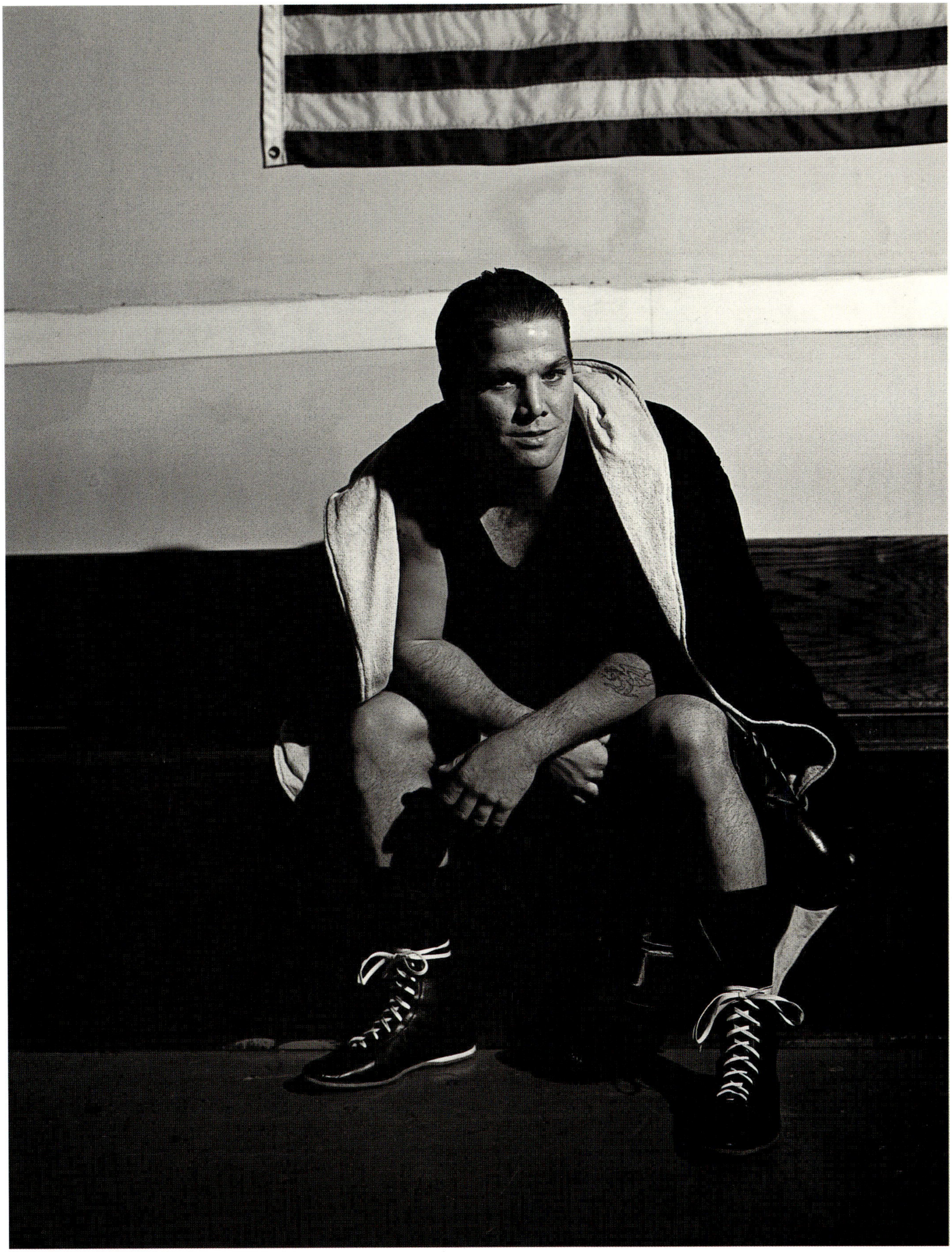

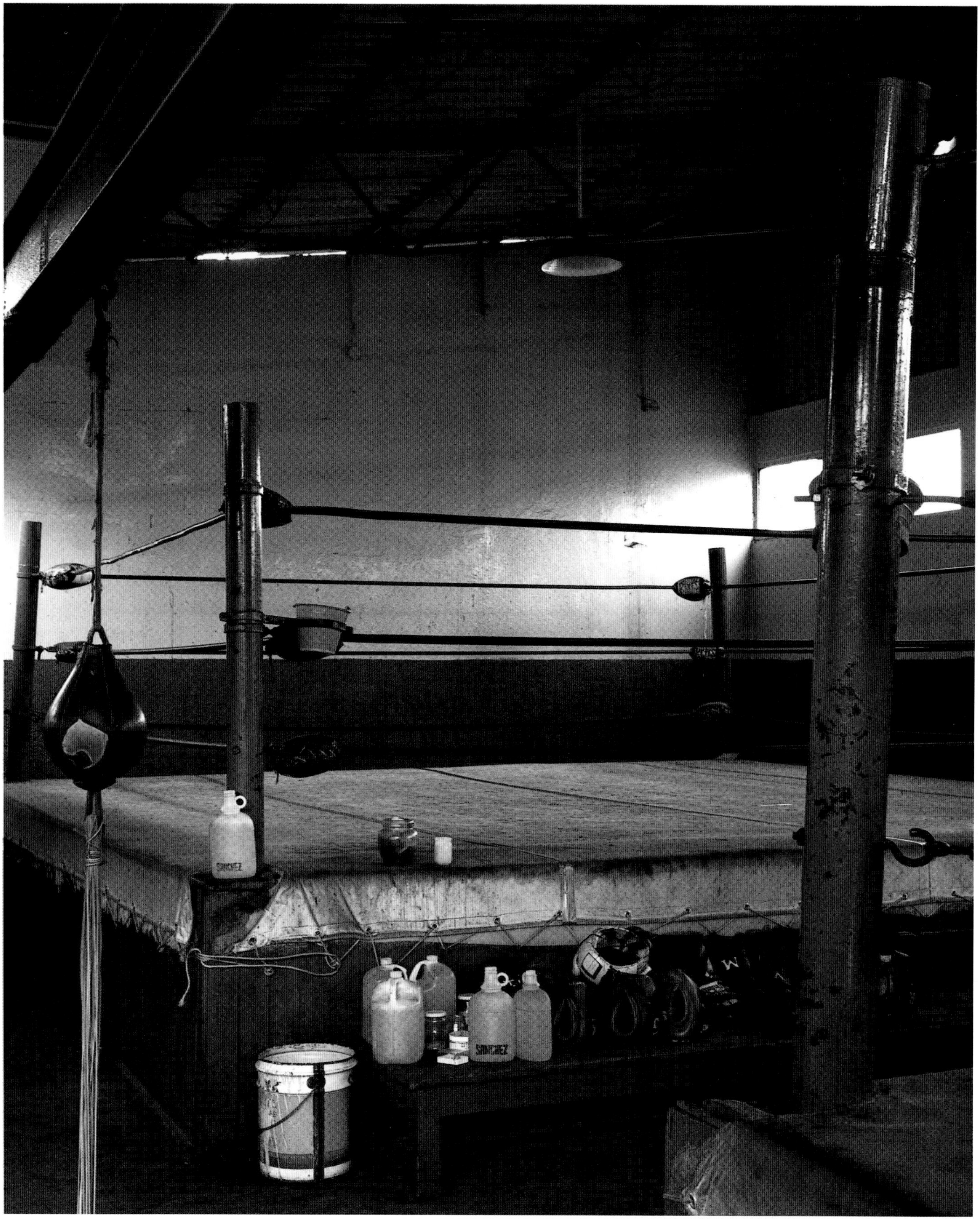
SANCHEZ
SANCHEZ

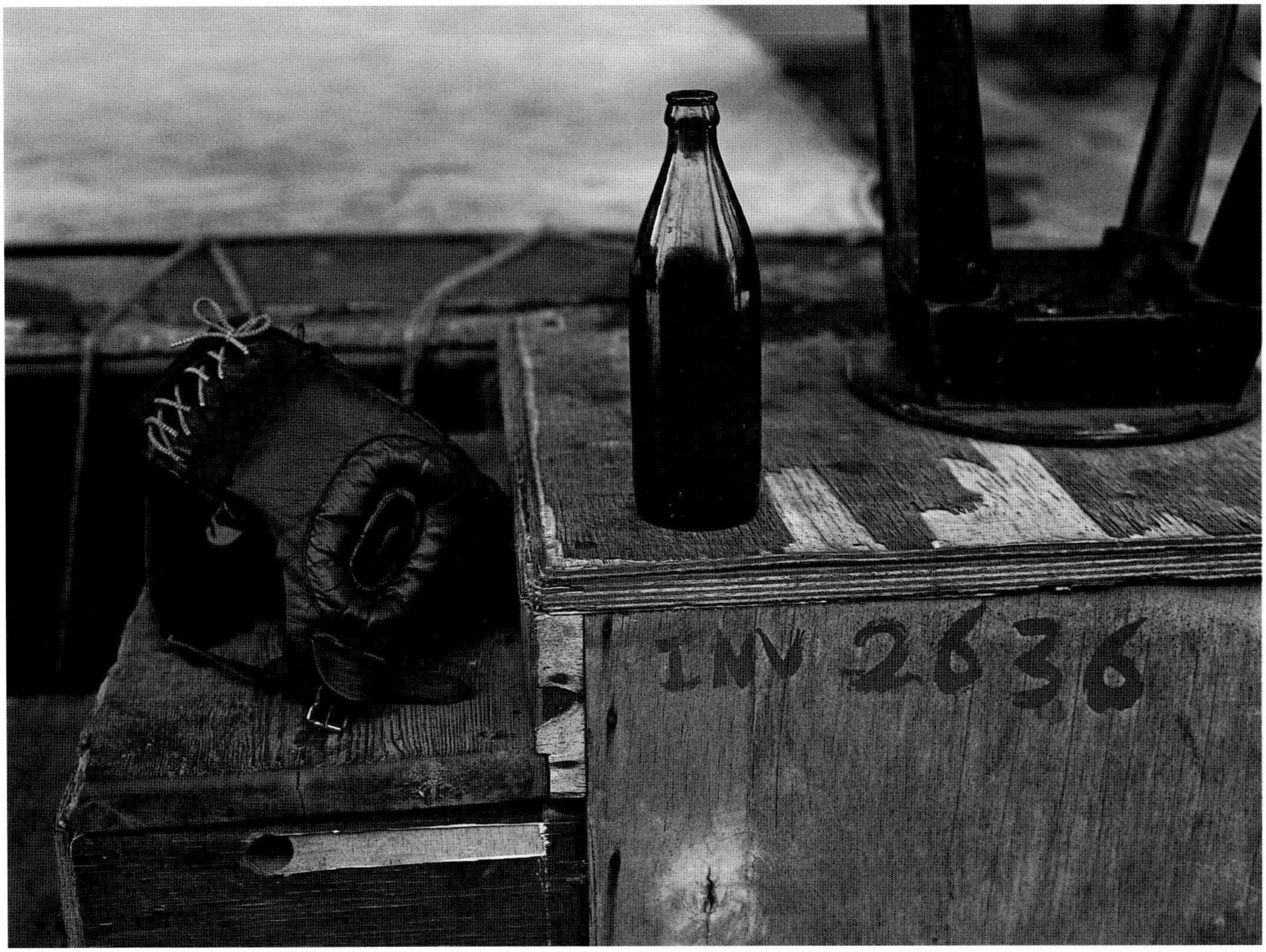
INV 2636

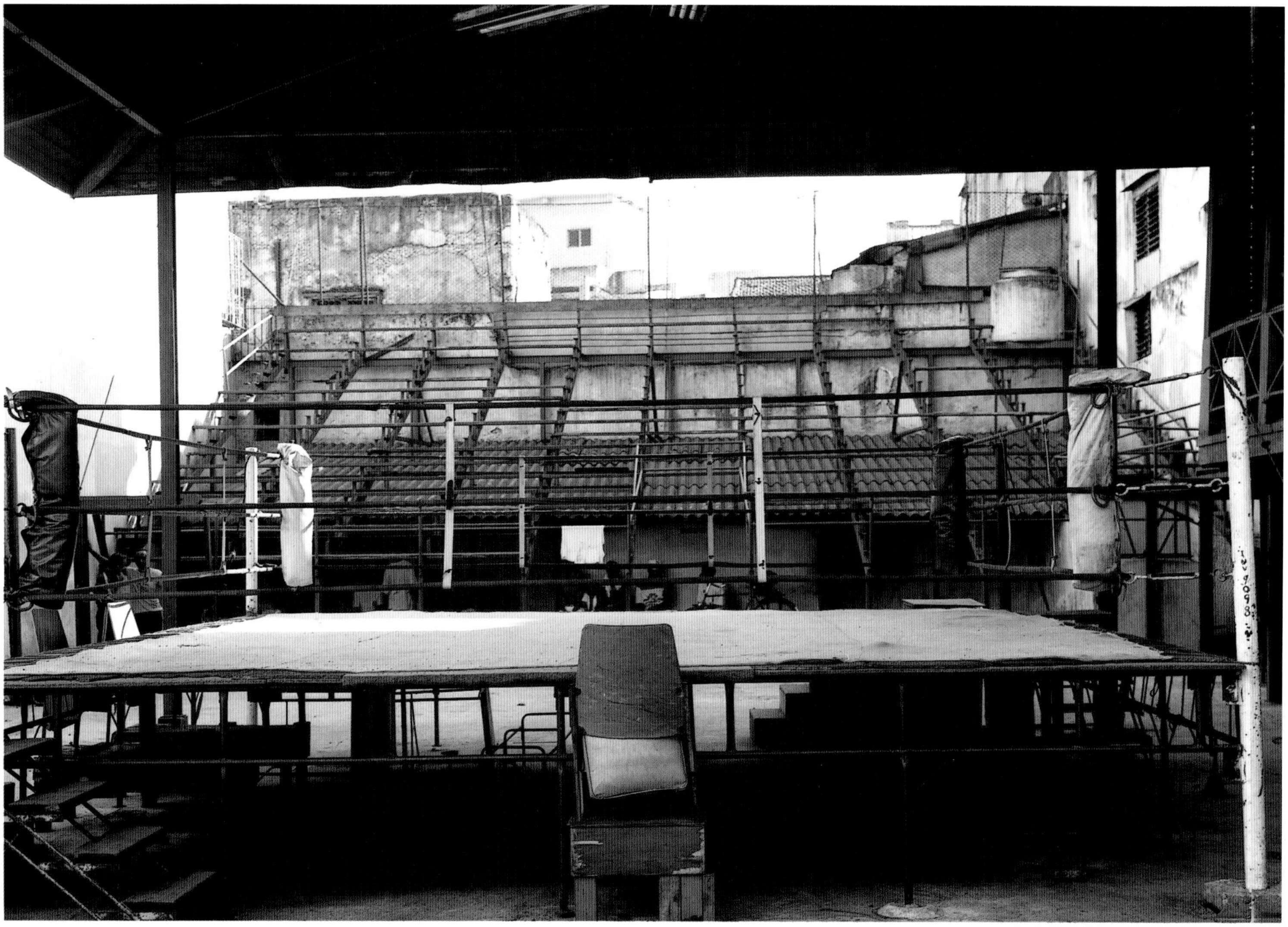

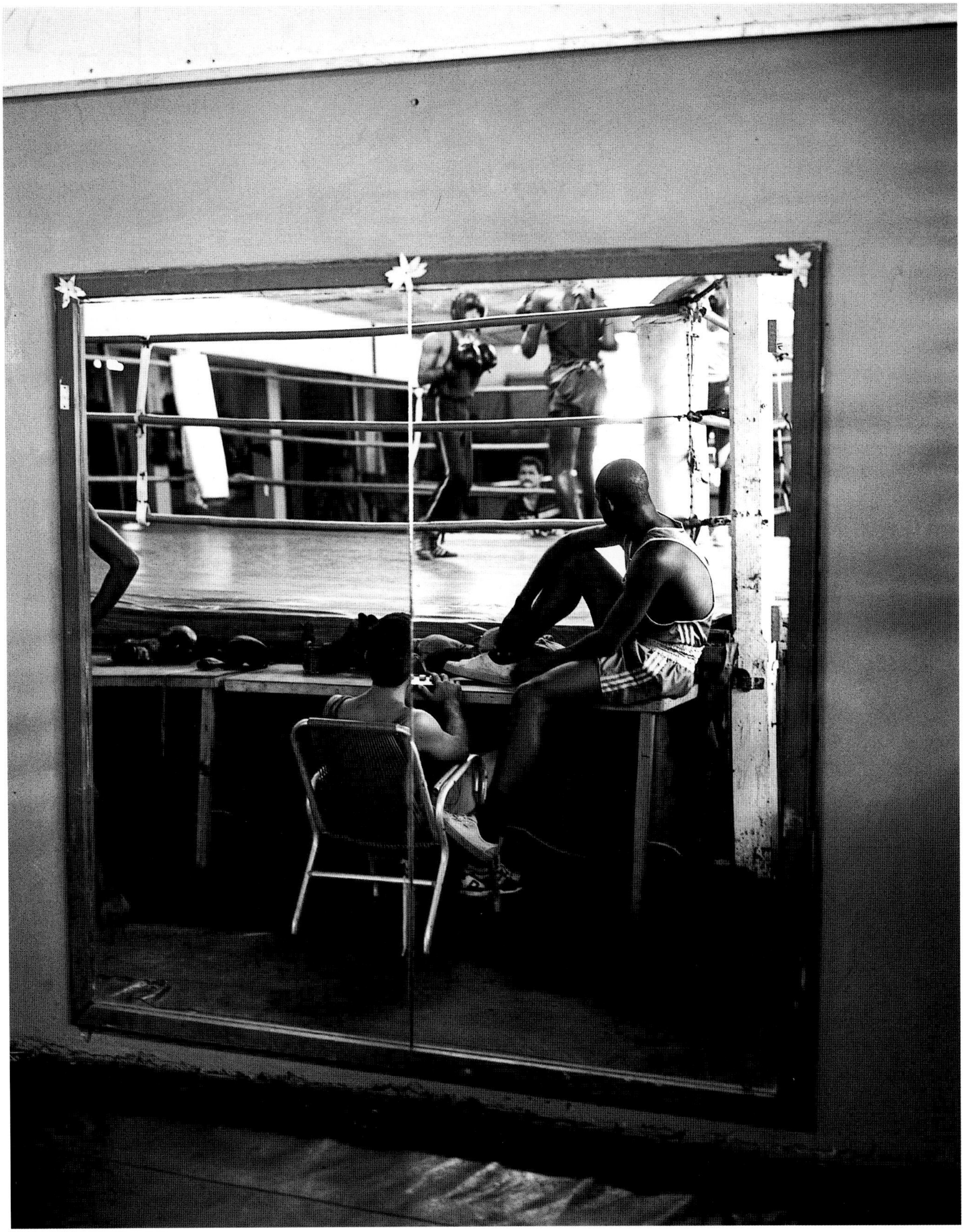

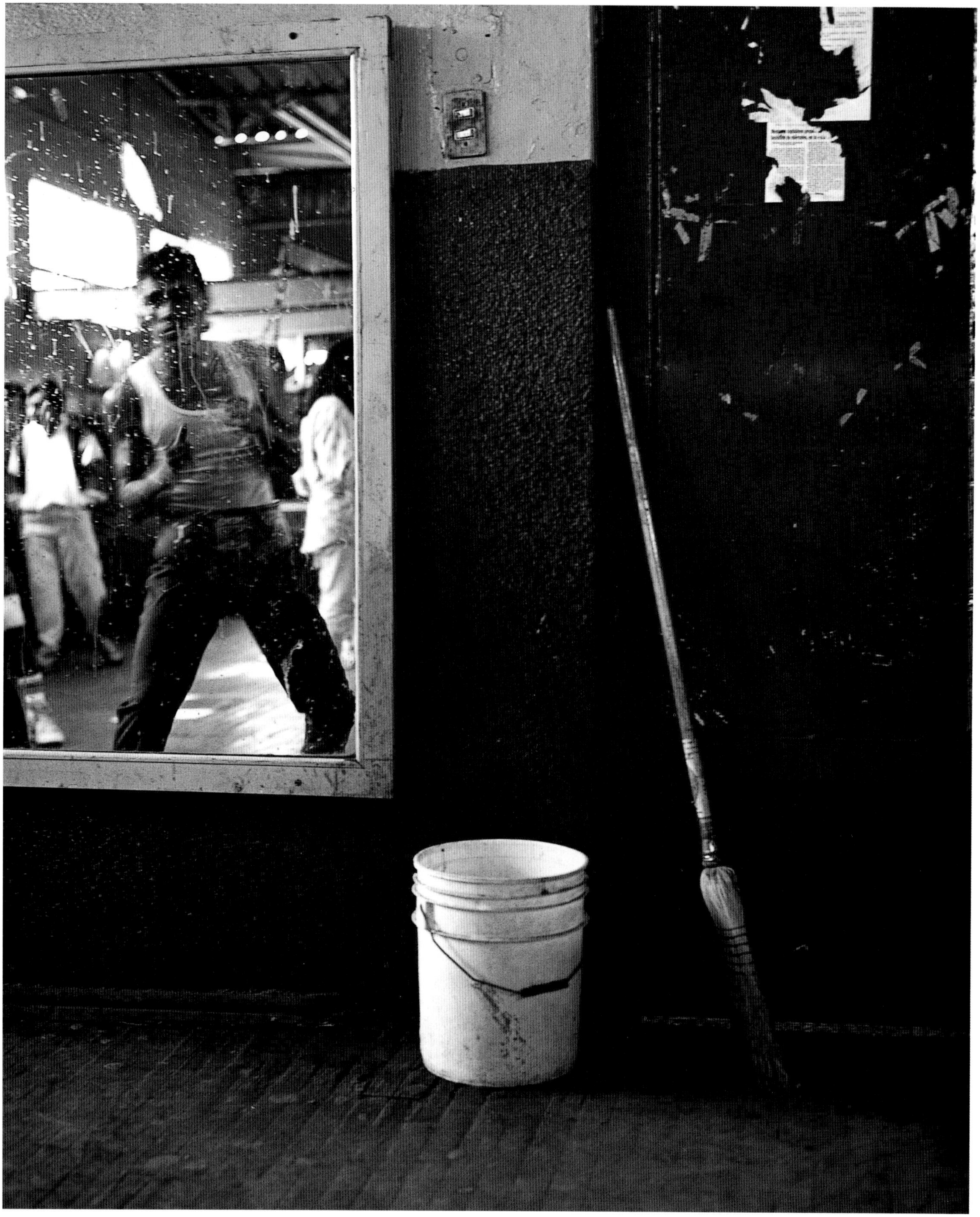

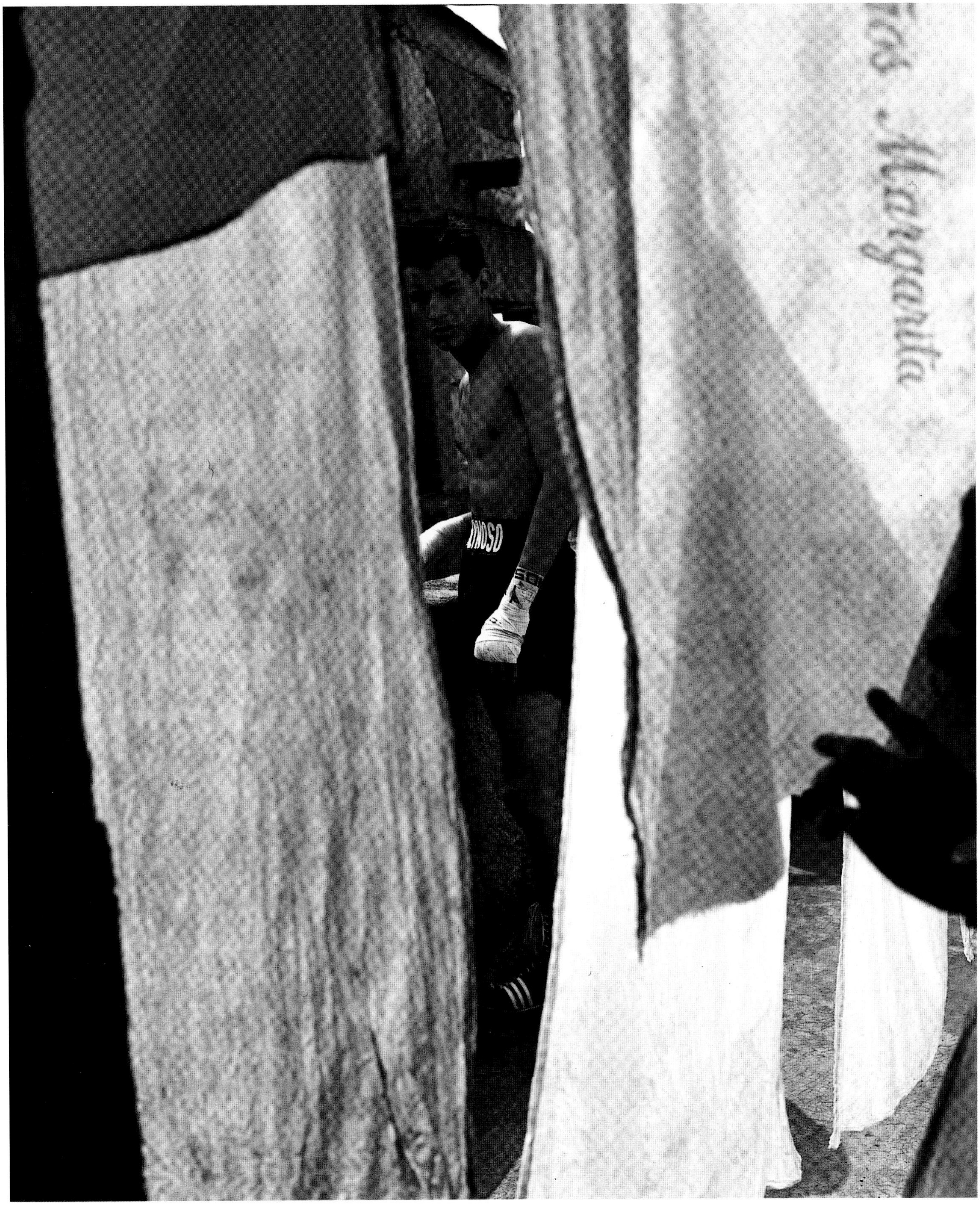
Margarita

Me, I'm her husband; she had a right to tell me to quit. Not the kid, she can't tell the kid what to do with his life; and he turned to look at his son in the ring.

NORMAN KATKOV

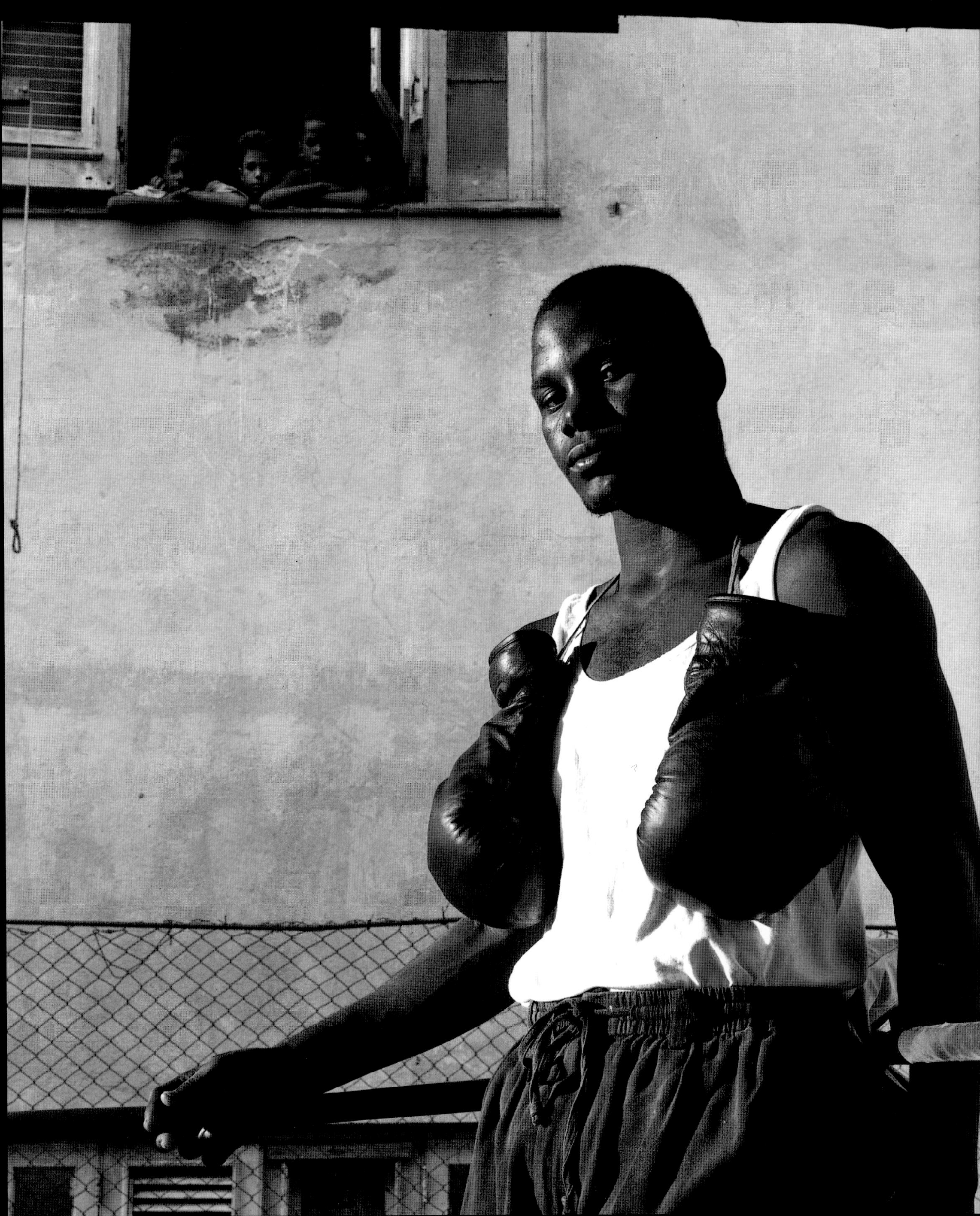

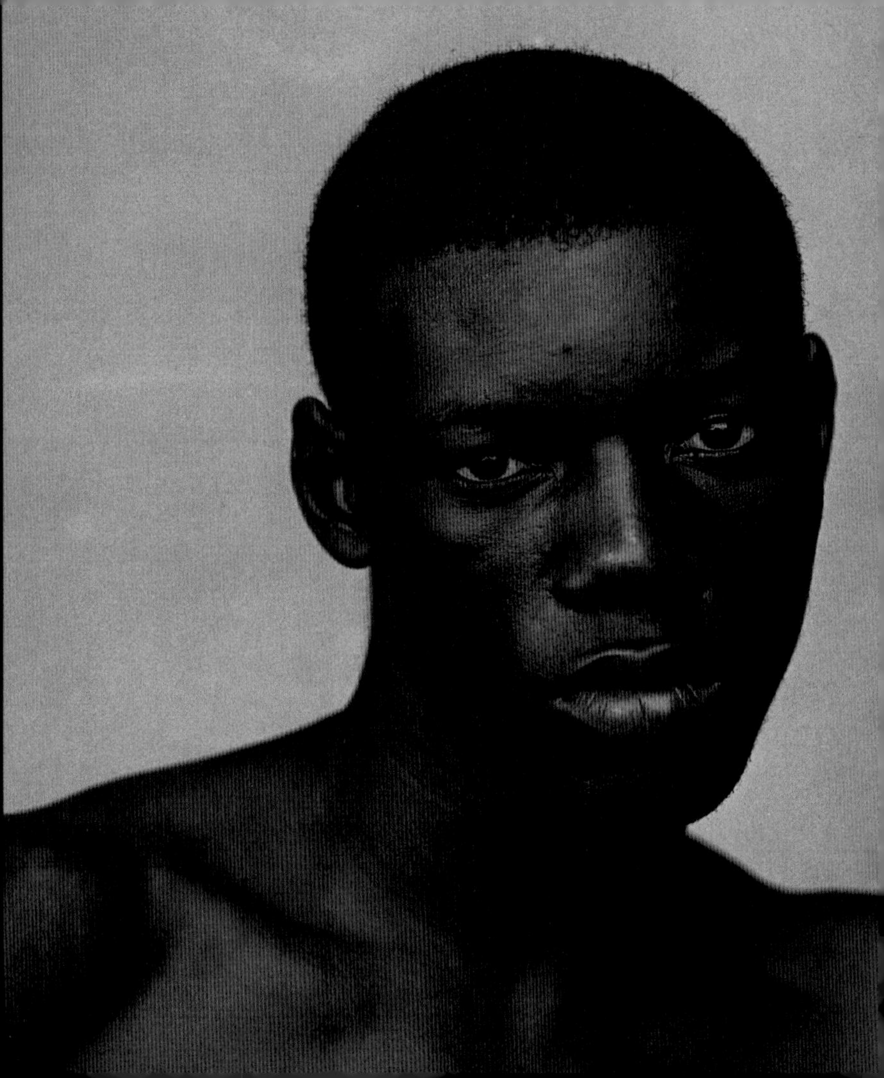

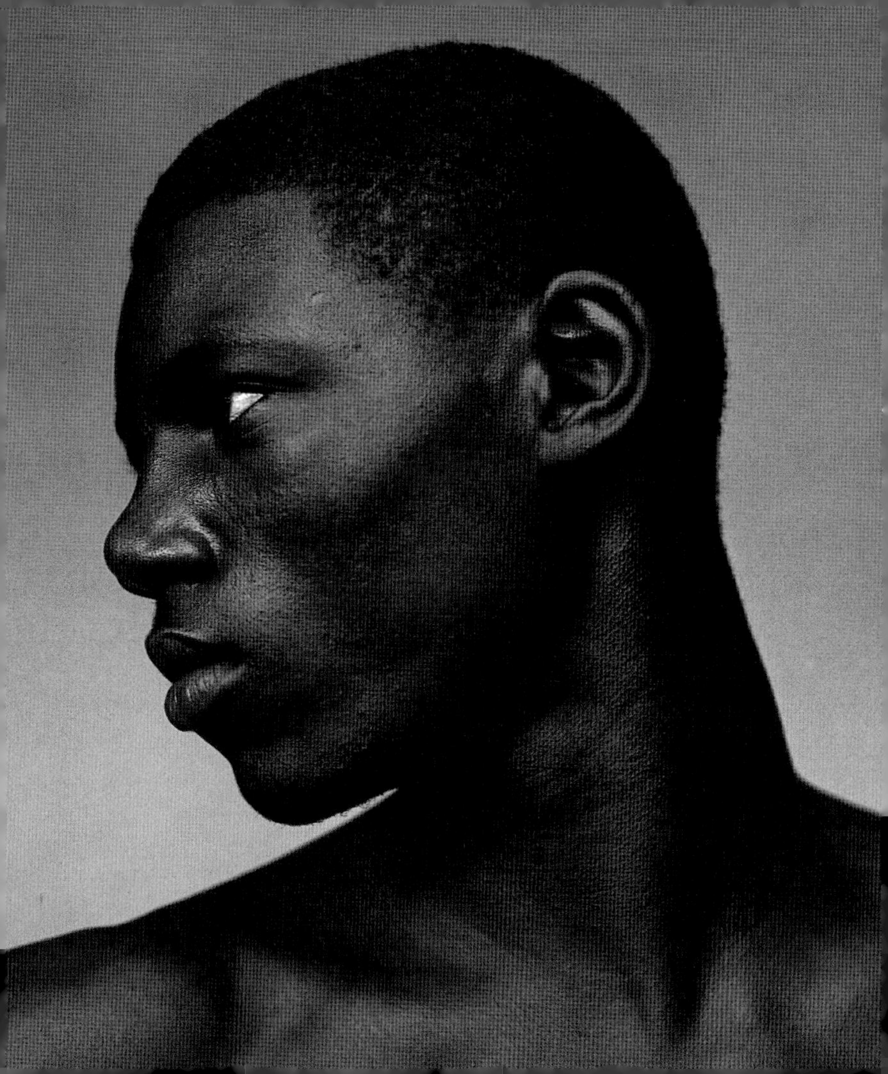

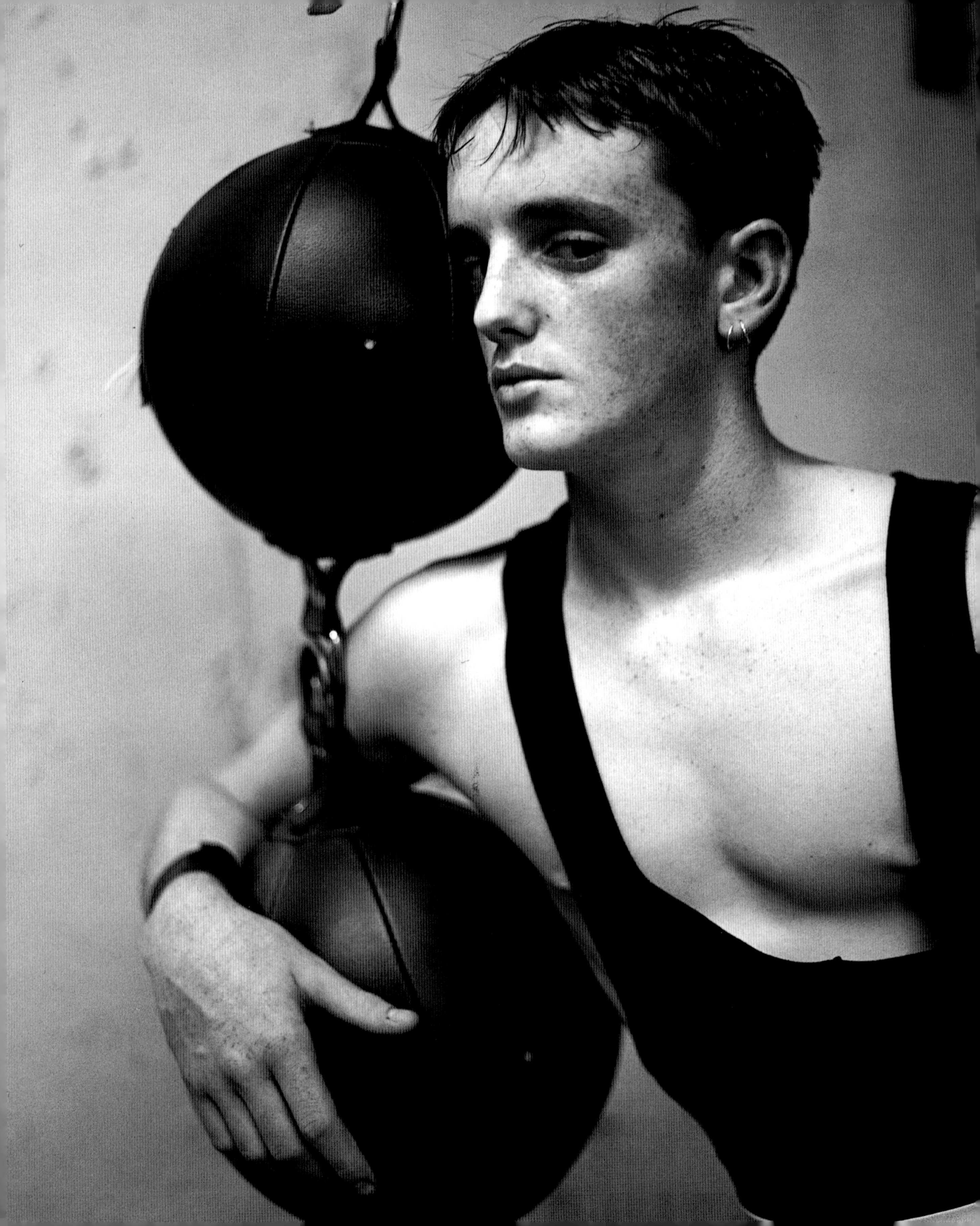

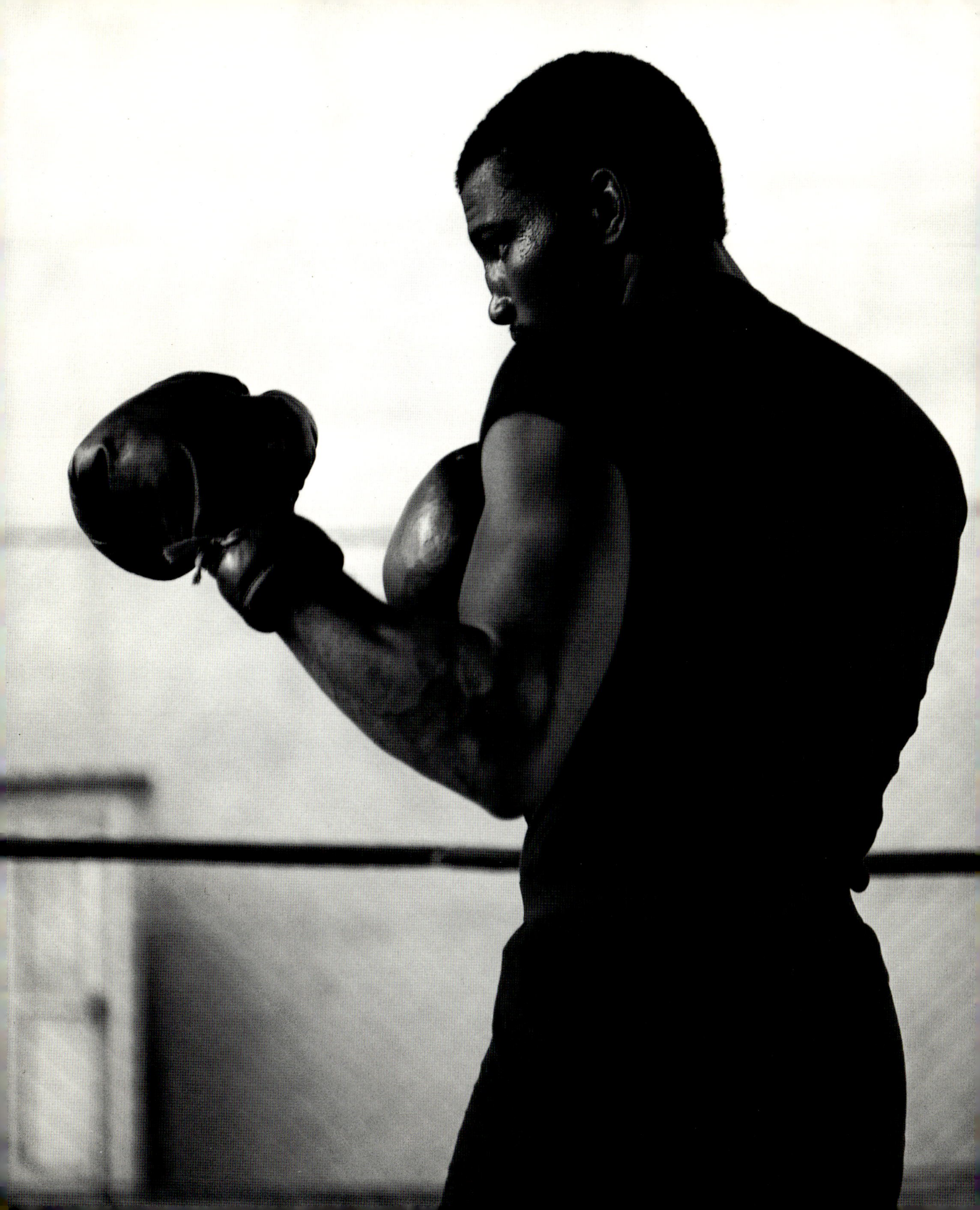

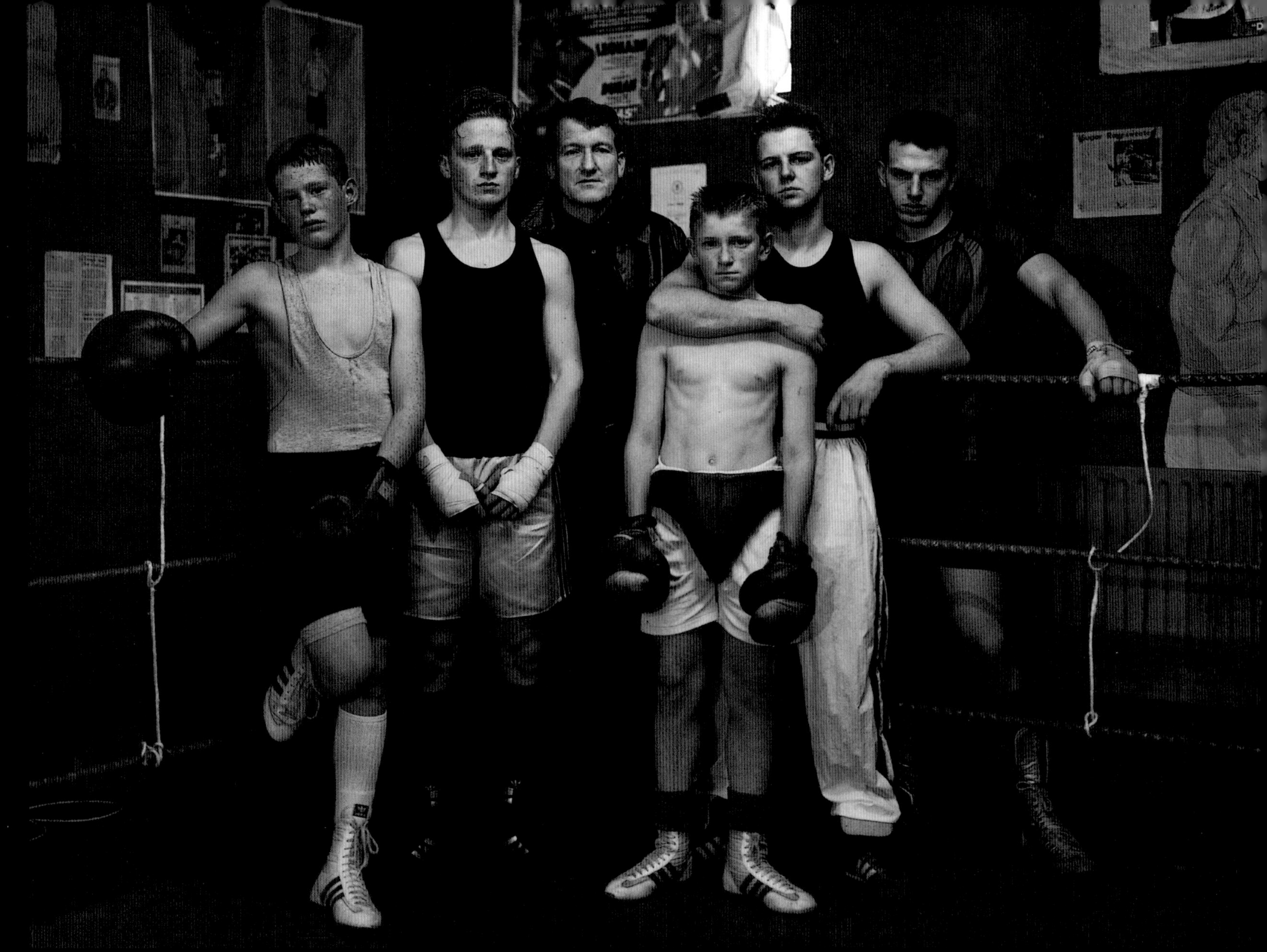

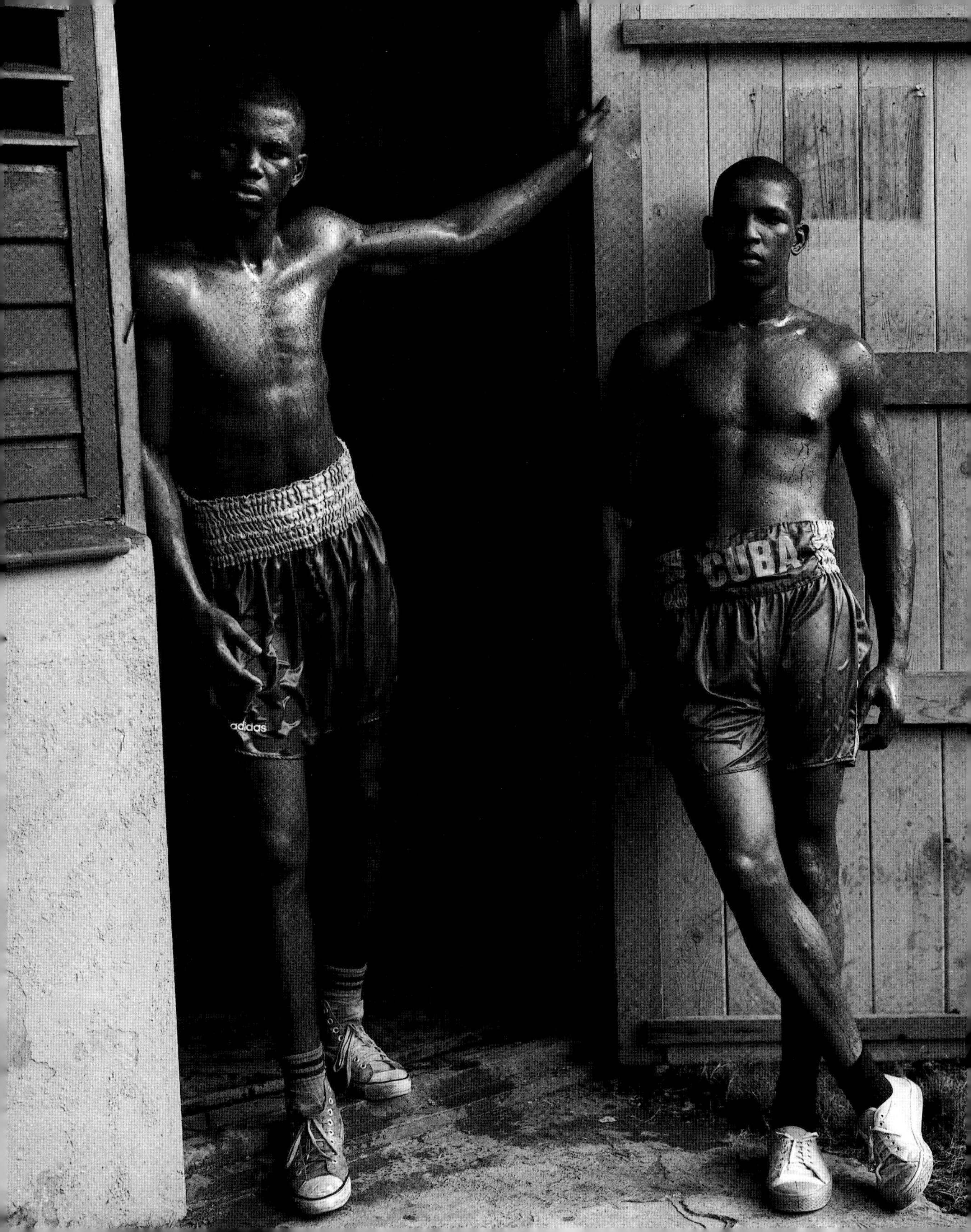
adidas
CUBA

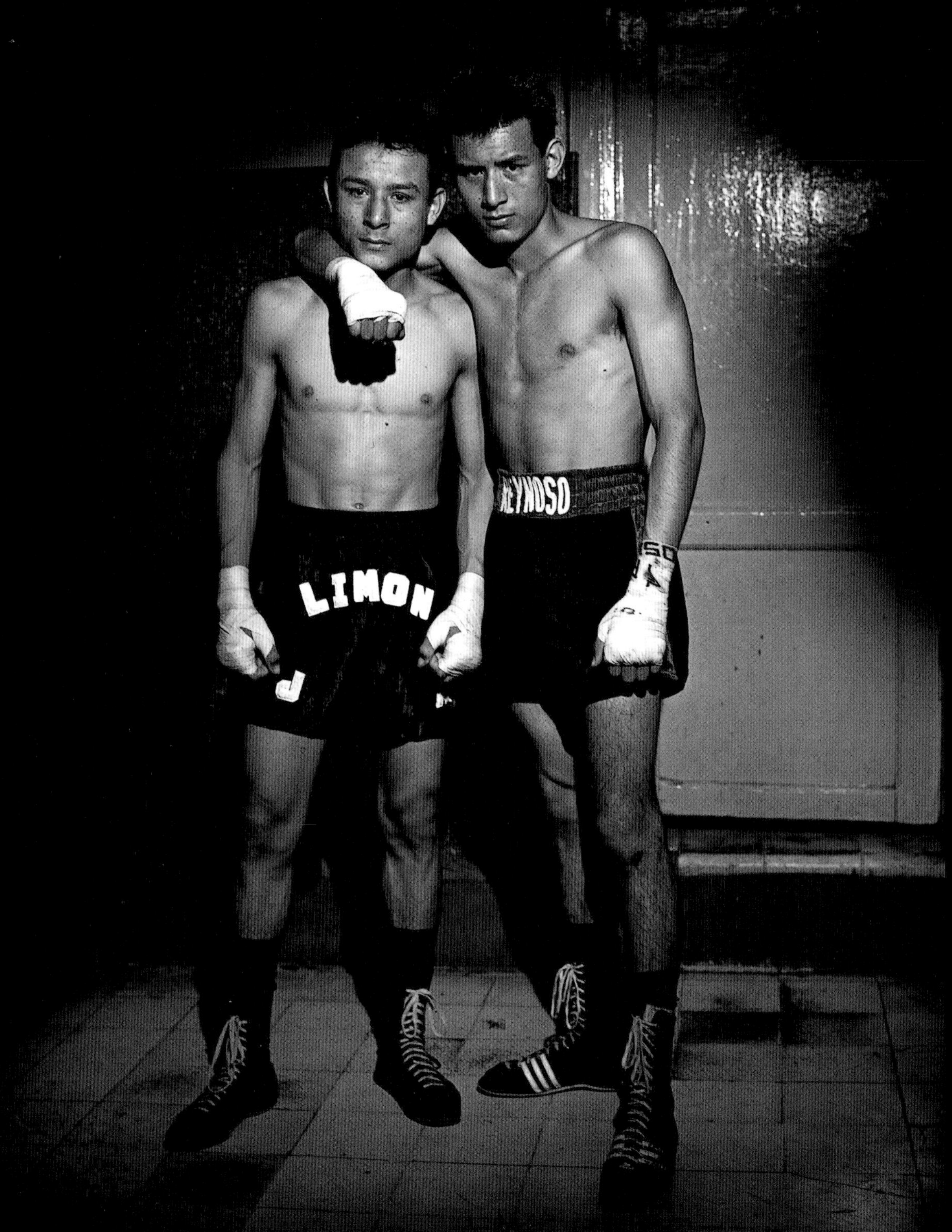
LIMON
REYNOSO

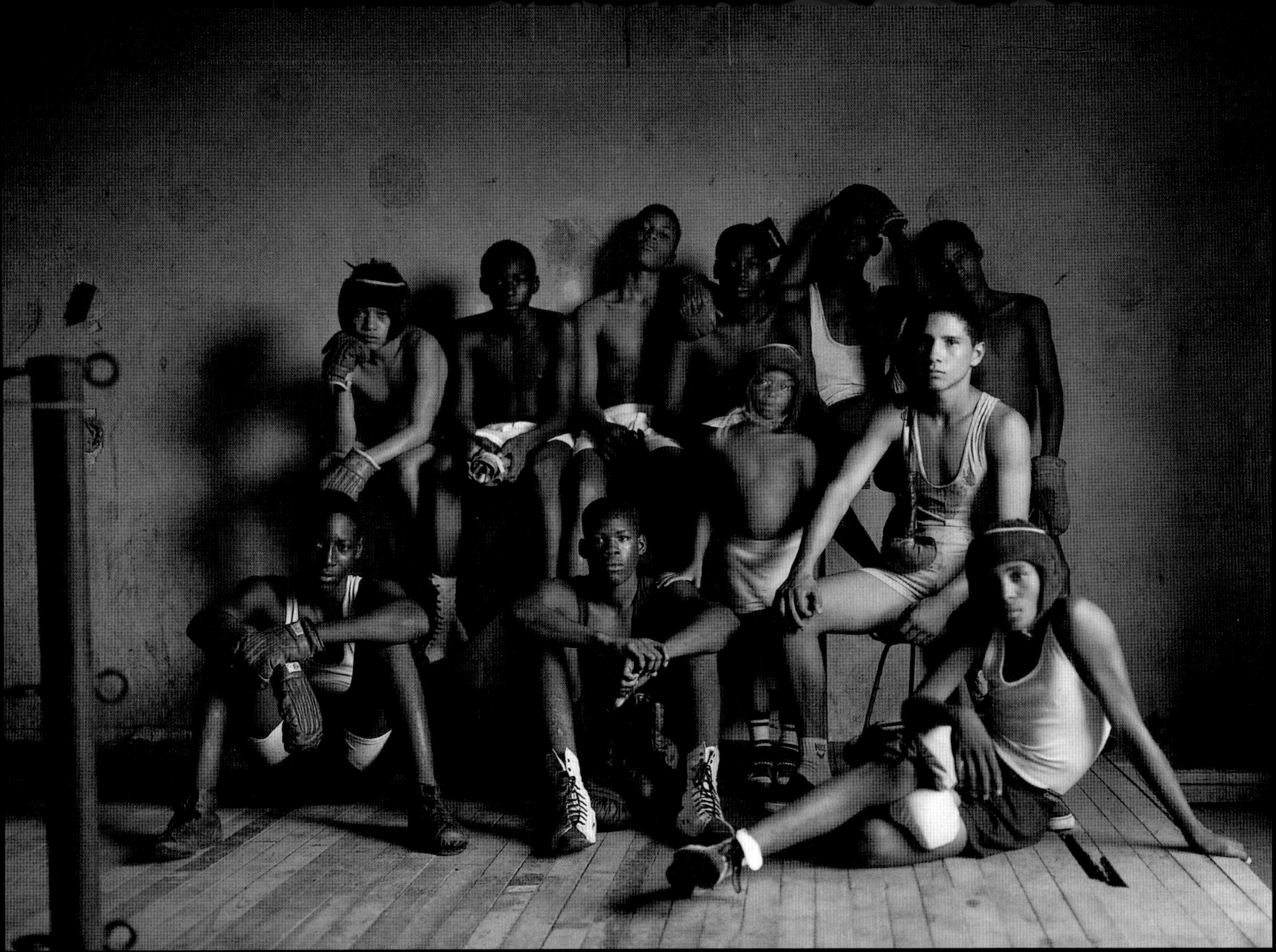

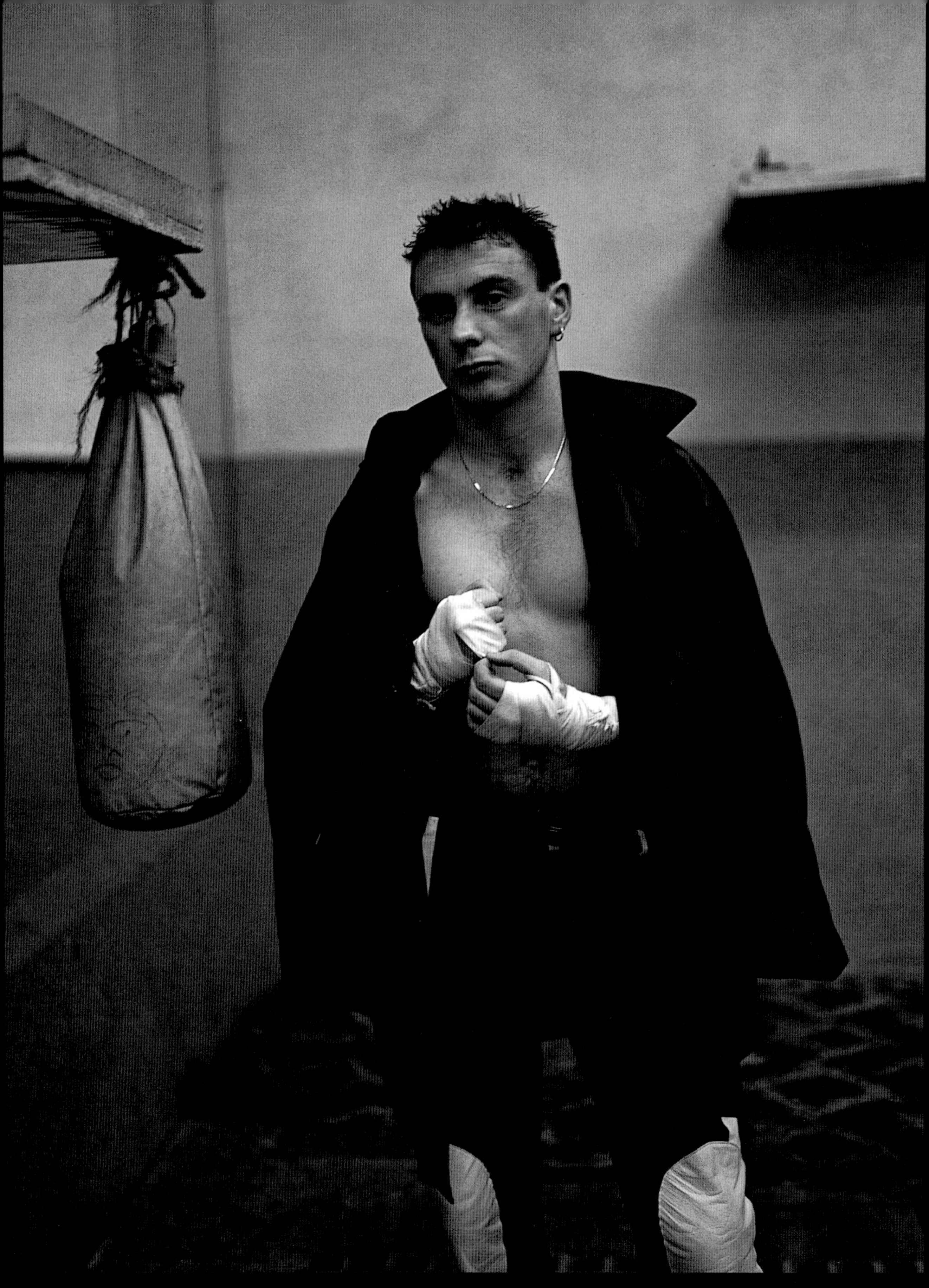

All I need's a fight and a woman. Then I'm set. I get the fight I'll get the money. I get the money I'll get the woman. There's some women that love you for yourself, but that don't last long.

LEONARD GARDNER

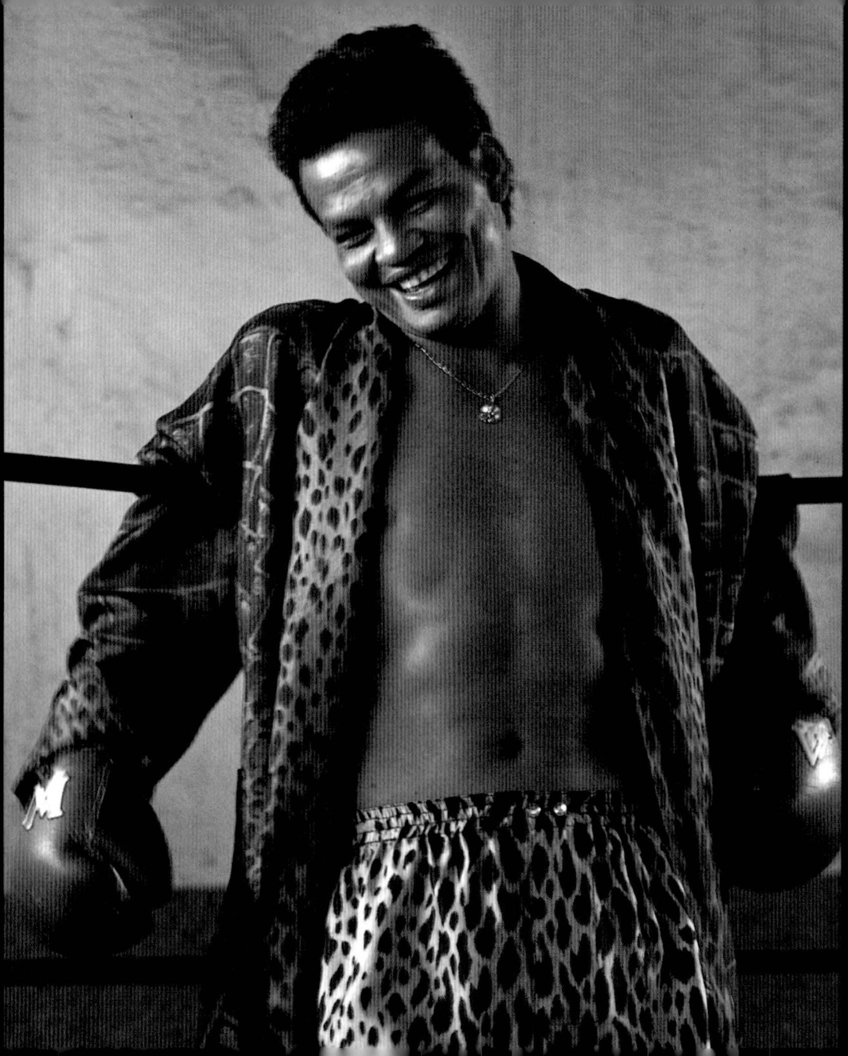

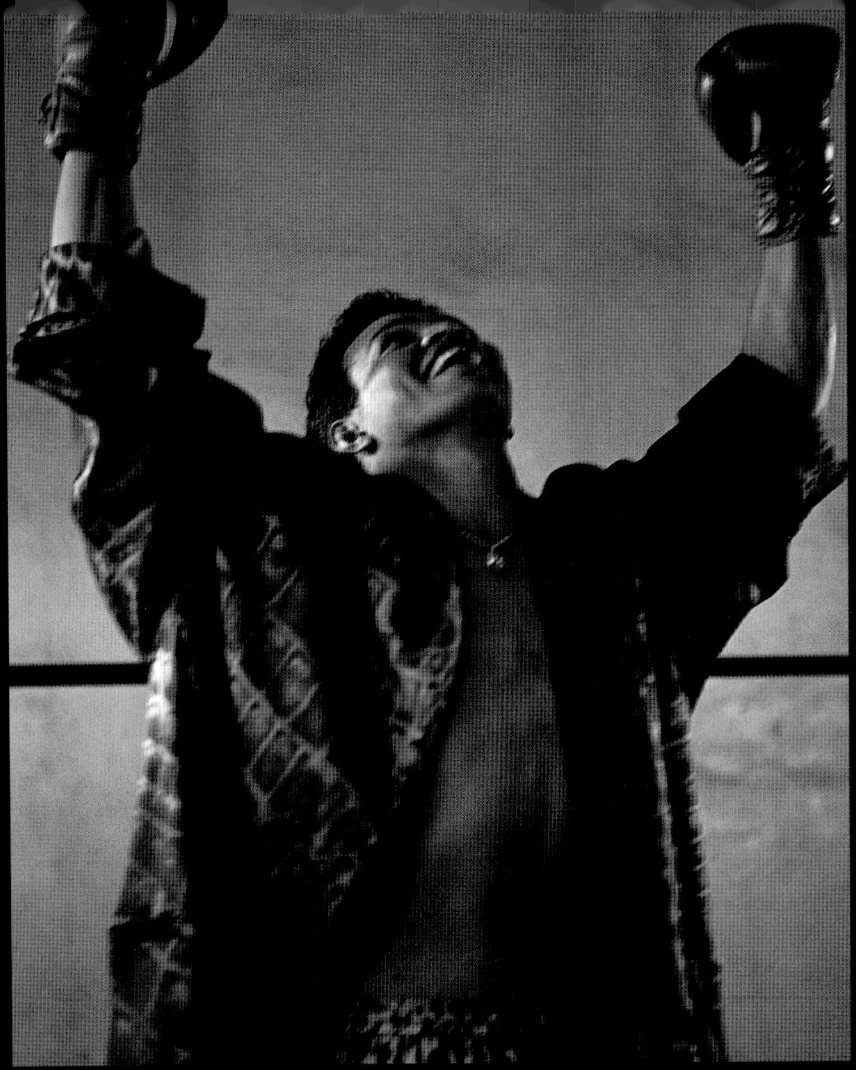

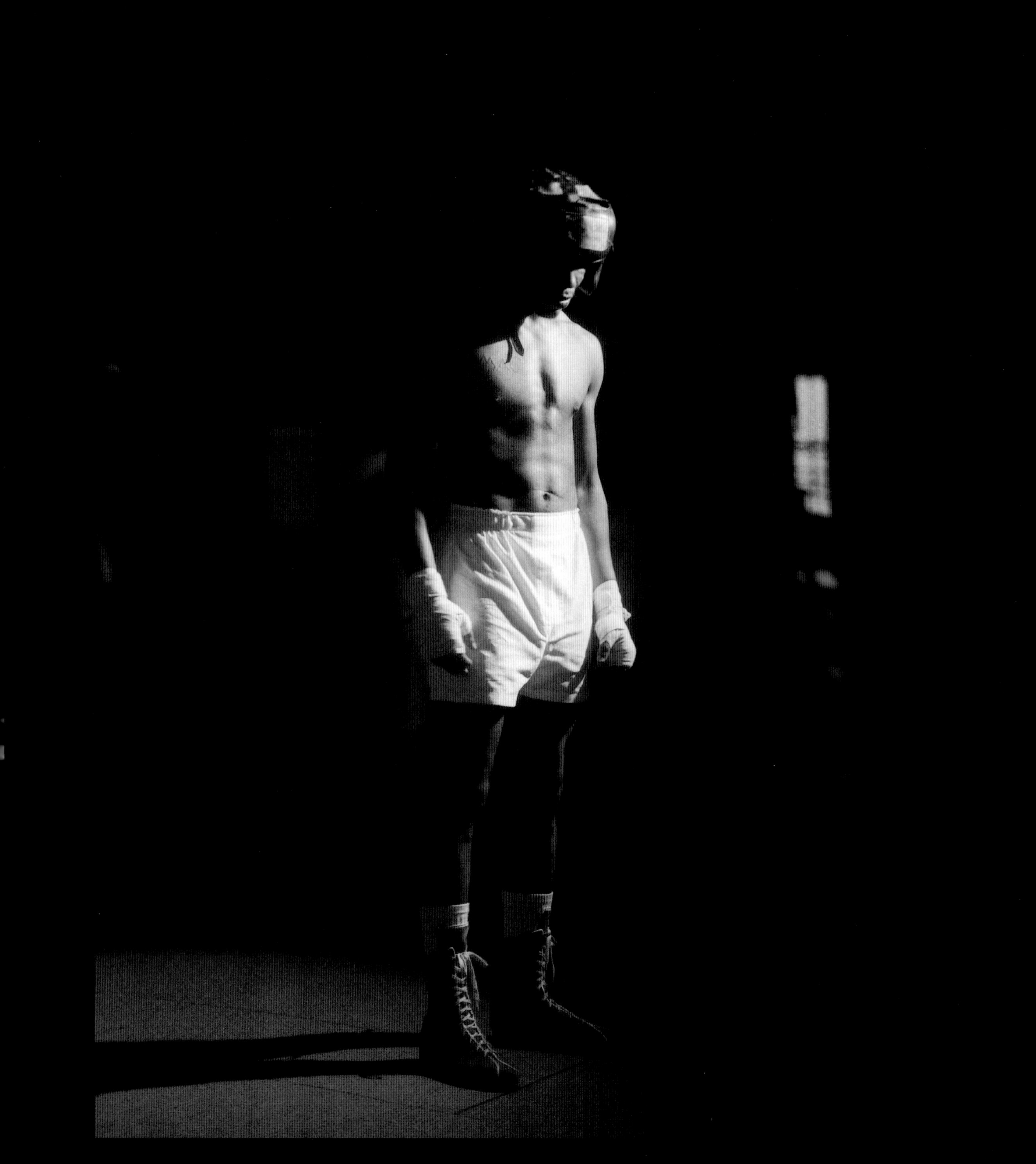

Then the man began to sing, repeating a single phrase, his voice rising from bass moans and bellows to falsetto wails. *Earth Angel, Earth Angel, will you be mine?* The song went on in the locker room, the singer, as he put on his clothes, shifting to an interlude of improvisation: *Baby, baaaby, baaaaby, uh baby, uuh, oh yeauh, BAAAAAAABY, I WANT YOU*, while naked figures walked to and from the showers and steam drifted through the doorway. Drawing on his pants, Ernie, bruised, fatigued and elated, felt he had joined the company of men.

LEONARD GARDNER

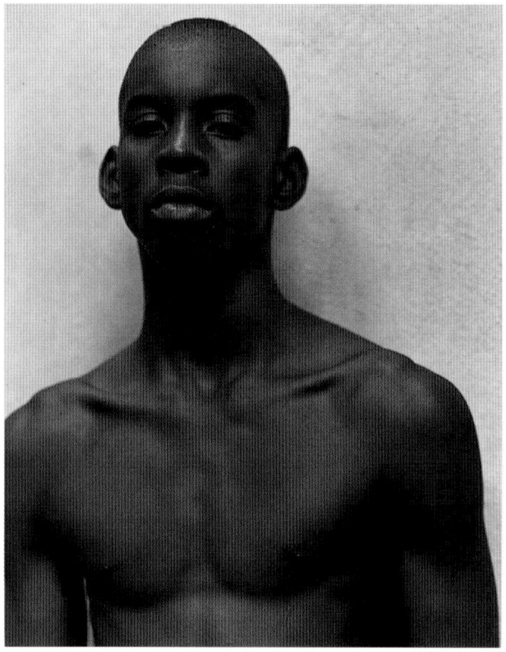

PLATES

35 Thomas Ennis, Dublin
36 Mexico City
37 Juan Carlos Igmus, Havana
38 Juan Cunba Beltran, Havana
39 Abbi Vega, Brooklyn
41 Alex Ramos, Brooklyn
42 Derek McConmack, Dublin
43 Dublin
44 Roberto Vidal, Mexico City
45 Havana
46 John Mondello, Brooklyn
47 Gustavo Baz, Mexico City
49 Brian Borzell, Brooklyn
50 Darren Power, Dublin
53 Dublin
55 Mexico City
57 Danny O'Reilly, Dublin
58 Jose Carmargo Medina, Mexico City
59 Jose Carmargo Medina, Mexico City
60 Mike Capriano, Brooklyn
61 Jimmy Burgese, Brooklyn
62 Guittermo Sandoval, Mexico City
63 Roberto Vidal, Mexico City
64 Mark Rock, Michael Rock, Dublin
65 Jose Carmargo Medina, Gregorio Medina, Mexico City
66 Sam Mitchell, Brooklyn
68 Dublin
69 Havana
70 Thomas Ennis, Dublin
71 Dublin
73 Havana
74 Mexico City
75 Andrez Gaspar, Havana
76 John Cullen, Dublin
77 Waldemar Font Quintera, Havana
79 Patrick Hyland, Dublin
80 Brooklyn
83 Mike Shephard, Brooklyn
84 Mexico City
85 Havana
86 Havana
87 Havana
88 Mexico City
89 Daniel Reynoso Hernandez, Mexico City
91 Ariel Hernandez Azcuy, Havana
92 Diosuany Vega Figugroa, Havana
93 Diosuany Vega Figugroa, Havana
94 Kristian Lokko, Dublin
95 Juan Carlos Igmus, Havana
96 Patrick Rogers, Thomas Ennis, John Dunne, Patrick West, David Kavanagh, Danny O'Reilly, Dublin
97 Juan Cunba Beltran, Fredy Roja, Havana
98 Jose Reynoso Hernandez, Daniel Reynoso Hernandez, Mexico City
99 Havana
100 Brian Lynch, Dublin
102 Marcos Villazana, Mexico City
103 Marcos Villazana, Mexico City
104 Sam Mitchell, Brooklyn
106 Damian Moraii, Havana
109 Juan Cunba Beltran, Havana
110 Kenneth Rock, Dublin

ACKNOWLEDGEMENTS

ROSS ALLISON
GIORGIO ARMANI
ROSANNA ARMANI
TOMMASO BASILIO
CLARE BERESFORD
NAN BUSH
SUSAN CLAIRE
BRENDA CORBIN
JACQUELINE DeGIOANNI
BRUNO Di DOMINICO
AURORA FERREYRA
ERIC GABRIEL
ANDY GEIGER
RIP GEORGES
POLLY HAMILTON
RICHARD KELLY
WALTER KIRN
DARREN LEW
VON LINDSAY
SUZY LINDSAY-MOORE
MARIA MARKUS
JOHN MATHER
ART O'BRIEN
JULIE ANNE QUAY
CHRISTIAN RAVERA
BRUCE SILVERGLADE
FELICIA SPECK
NICOLE TAVENNER
LYNN TESORO
SEIKO UYEDA
BRUCE WEBER
JACK WOODY

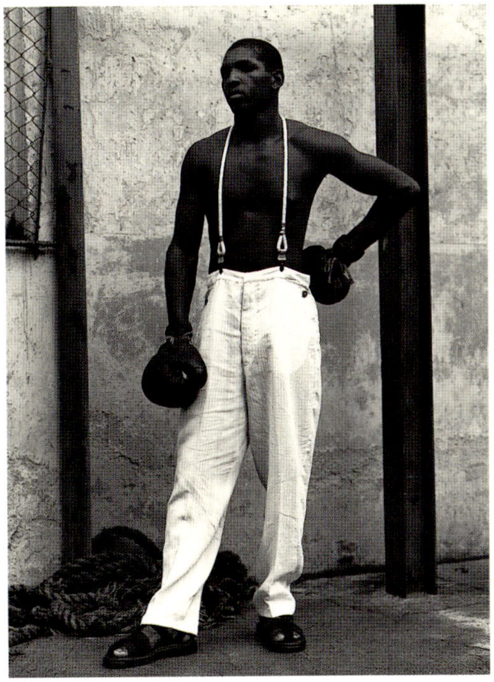

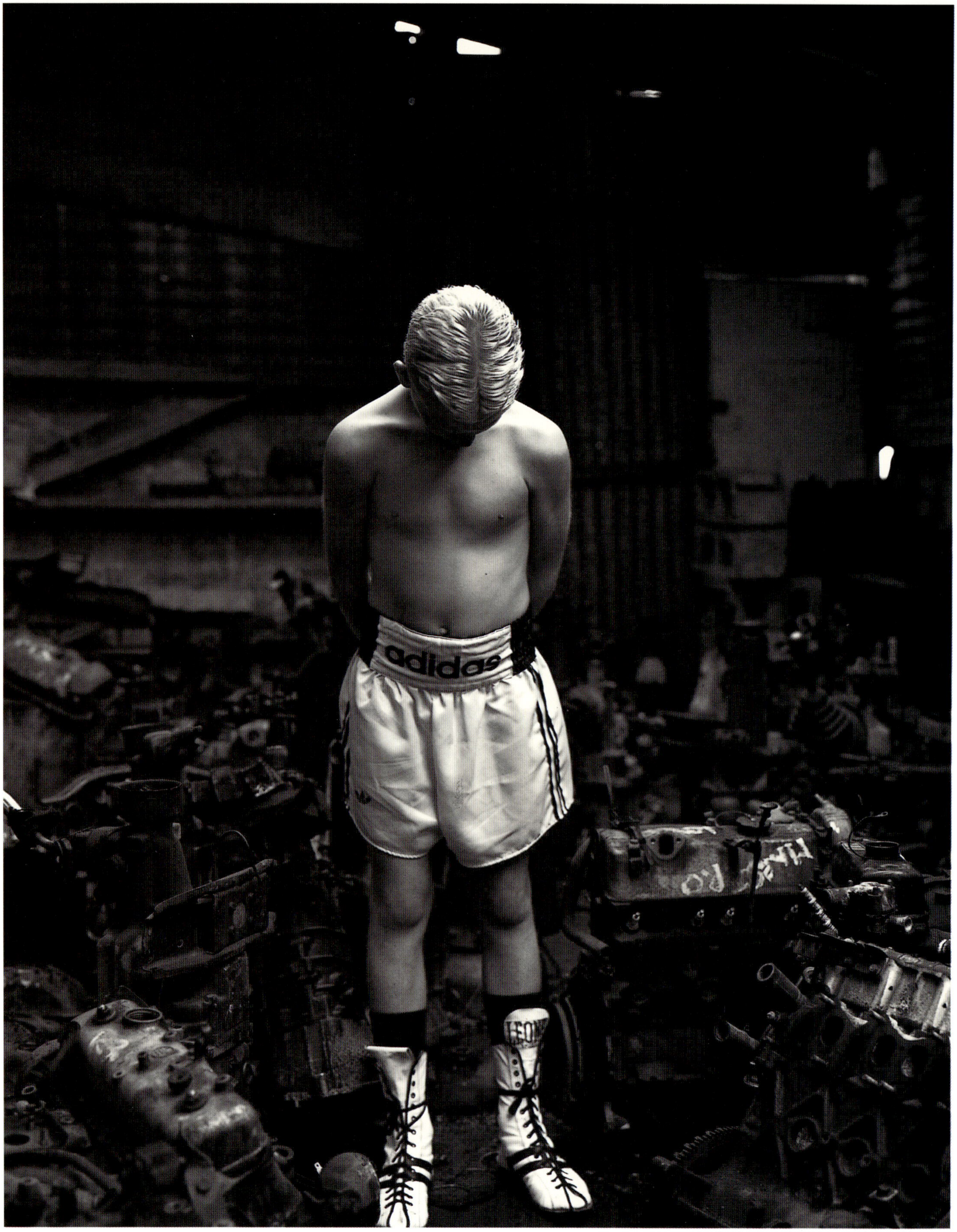
adidas

FOR MARIA AND ERIC

COLOPHON

This first edition of *Boxers* is limited to 4000 casebound copies and 150 slipcased, autographed and numbered special edition copies. Book design is by Kurt Markus with Von Lindsay. Printed and bound in Hong Kong by Palace Press International for: Twin Palms Publishers, Post Office Box 10229 Santa Fe, New Mexico 87504, 505 988-5717. www.twinpalms.com

ISBN 0-944092-36-5 REGULAR EDITION

ISBN 0-944092-37-3 LIMITED EDITION

1998